What Your Pediatrician Doesn't Know Can Hurt Your Child

What Your Pediatrician Doesn't Know Can Hurt Your Child

A More Natural Approach to Parenting

SUSAN MARKEL, MD

WITH LINDA F. PALMER

BENBELLA BOOKS, INC.
Dallas, Texas

Copyright © 2010 by Susan Markel

BenBella Books, Inc.
10300 N. Central Expressway, Suite 400
Dallas, TX 75231
www.benbellabooks.com
Send feedback to feedback@benbellabooks.com

Printed in the United States of America
10 9 8 7 6 5 4 3 2 1

Library of Congress Cataloging-in-Publication Data is available for this title.
ISBN 978-1-935618-10-2

Copyediting by Paul Eisenberg
Proofreading by Erica Lovett and Greg Teague
Index by Tracy Wilson-Burns
Cover design by Faceout
Text design and composition by John Reinhardt Book Design
Printed by Bang Printing

Distributed by Perseus Distribution
(www.perseusdistribution.com)

To place orders through Perseus Distribution:
Tel: 800-343-4499
Fax: 800-351-5073
E-mail: orderentry@perseusbooks.com

Significant discounts for bulk sales are available.
Please contact Glenn Yeffeth at glenn@benbellabooks.com or (214) 750-3628.

Contents

SECTION THREE
MAINTAINING HEALTH

Some Words from the Author

The Pronoun Problem

In our language, the lack of a neutral third-person singular for humans is certainly problematic in a book where the author is trying to be general, not referring specifically to girls or boys. In conventional English usage, the masculine "he" and "him" are used except in situations where the subject clearly refers to a female.

Although clearly the default "he" might disturb half the population, the same might be said every time that "she" were used to include both genders.

Given that the English language cannot be completely rewritten, and also that contrived phrases such as "he or she" and he/she are best avoided, in this book the masculine is used except in situations where the subject is clearly a female—which is about half the time anyway, because naturally "she" and "her" are used when referring to the mother. So while some might argue that traditional language fails to reflect the presence of women and girls, the feminist point of view might well be that when the situation is specifically female, attention must be paid, because females are "exceptional" rather than the basic default "everybody."

About the Book

This book is organized into three parts. The first section addresses things that you would like to know from day one as a parent, the second focuses on behavior and relationships, and the third part takes what you've learned and applies it to your child's health as time goes on. You'll find education and encouragement in these pages so that you'll not only be able to confidently nurture your child, but you'll be able to do so in a highly respectful way. There's no stopping you from exceeding all of your expectations as a parent once you see yourself as the ultimate expert in raising your own child.

Introduction

DOCTORS ARE TRAINED to diagnose disease and use pharmaceutical drugs, and that's how they practice. They are not formally trained in health or nutrition, so asking your pediatrician for advice on either nutrition or health—meaning how to keep your child as healthy as possible—will probably be useless unless your doctor has been self-taught. If you've educated yourself in these matters it's likely that you'll know as much or more about them than your child's doctor.

Nor are doctors educated about natural parenting or natural lifestyles—the benefits of sleeping with your baby versus having your baby "cry it out" in a crib, or the benefits of carrying your baby in a wrap, sling, or other soft carrier versus leaving the baby in a hard plastic baby-containing contraption.

A few hard truths about many of the pediatricians practicing today...

- They may say things that are not scientifically justified. It's fascinating that so many long-held beliefs in pediatrics are ultimately refuted by carefully done studies.
- They may be advising based on their own opinion or prejudice.
- They may be prescribing out of routine, convenience, or habit.

- They might be telling you what they think you want to hear, even if they internally disagree.
- Their decisions may be affected by the dictates of insurance companies, drug companies, or state and federal governments.

Some other things you may not know…

- Once your child is born, it is not necessary for the hospital to take your baby to the nursery to be bathed and weighed.
- Also while at the hospital, your baby does *not* necessarily need:
  - A vitamin injection;
  - A vaccine against hepatitis;
  - Eye drops to prevent infection;
  - Formula supplementation "just to be sure" in case you can't produce enough breast milk;
  - Water supplementation if your baby is jaundiced.
- Babies who are breast-fed are healthier than those who are artificially fed.
- Although car seats are critical while your baby's in a car, at all other times your child ought to be held close to your body in a soft carrier rather than being pushed around in any kind of stroller.
- It's healthy and often desirable to sleep with your baby.
- Your baby is probably not underweight, no matter what your pediatrician's growth chart says.
- Milk is not an important source of calcium.
- You cannot "spoil" an infant by responding to his every need.
- Your toddler's "misbehavior" does not need to be punished.
- Boys who have trouble paying attention should not necessarily be medicated.
- Allergies and asthma can be prevented or helped considerably with methods other than medication.
- Eczema flare-ups should not be controlled simply by the use of steroid creams.
- Ear infections can be prevented, and when they occur, they can they be cured without medical intervention.
- Fever need not be controlled with fever-reducing medication.

- Most children's illnesses go away on their own, often faster without medical treatment.
- Your child need not receive all available childhood vaccines, on schedule.
- Your child should get plenty of time in healthy sunshine.

Given that many doctors either don't know these things or choose not to address them as alternatives, it follows that you as a parent may need to begin questioning the advice that you're getting from your pediatrician. You've probably already been told something by a doctor that betrays your own intuition. Rather than adhering unquestioningly to a doctor's authority, question it—after all, you're paying for the service. You have an absolute right to know why you're being asked to do something that relates to your child's health as well as how your doctor's recommendations and decisions may affect each other. Parents who question are taking active responsibility for their child's health.

Parents who question are taking active responsibility for their child's health.

Nothing is more frightening for a parent than having a sick child. Your job is to find a physician who's sympathetic to your concerns as well as knowledgeable enough to know what's serious and requires treatment, and what doesn't. If you're seeking a more holistic healthcare model, you'll want to find a pediatrician who considers your wishes. The most valuable pediatrician, quite simply, is the one who understands you and your child, who doesn't push the use of ineffective and potentially harmful drug treatments, and who respects your efforts to build and nurture your child's body and spirit *your way*.

In an age of "modern medicine," where there's a pill for every malady and a name for every human condition, we can't lose the ability to take care of ourselves and our families. Some aspects of contemporary medicine have done more harm than good, and while it can be daunting for you to even think about doubting the advice of a medical professional or any expert, you ultimately are in charge. You

DOCTORS HAVE DIVIDED LOYALTIES

Parents look to doctors to be healers, heroes, miracle workers, advocates, friends, spiritual guides, and educators. For the most part, doctors do act for the benefit of their patients. However, doctors also have a responsibility to society as a whole (and his or her other patients) and this might influence the manner in which decisions are made for your child.

---

are not ignorant. You are not helpless. You have good instincts, and so does your baby. Beyond instinct, you can educate yourself to raise your child in the best possible way. Nobody is better qualified.

Doctors trained in traditional Western medicine who have studied for years and have a degree need not be authoritarian. They can still respect your point of view and be open if you wish to discuss alternative ideas. While your pediatrician is likely competent in issues of illness, injury, and emergency care, he might not be as well-versed in breast-feeding, co-sleeping, natural remedies, and behavioral issues.

It's not hard to find qualified pediatricians who are well trained at the best institutions and stay on top of the latest research and trends in medicine. *The challenge is to find a doctor who is not totally bound to tradition.* An enlightened pediatrician knows when to prescribe medicine and, more importantly, when not to. A truly empathetic pediatrician will listen to your concerns thoughtfully and sympathize with you when appropriate, but will always, above all else, be your child's advocate.

Your pediatrician need not scare you. When your child is sick, the pediatrician should tell you what is truly the best course of action, which might be nothing more than measures to make your child more comfortable while nature takes its course. Restraint and reassurance may well be the best remedy despite the parents' and the doctor's inclination to "do something." Similarly, during well-child visits your pediatrician should be offering mainly encouragement and support—noting that your baby is doing exactly what he should be doing at that particular stage

Confidence in your pediatrician comes from having one who listens to you, genuinely cares about your child, and will do everything possible that's in keeping with your own beliefs about what constitutes a healthy lifestyle. Chances are that if you feel comfortable talking openly and freely to your pediatrician, then eventually your child will feel the same way.

DISCOVERY

"The more people have studied different methods
of bringing up children the more they have come
to the conclusion that what good mothers
and fathers instinctively feel like doing
for their babies is the best after all."

—BENJAMIN SPOCK

1

From Birth Onward, Every Procedure Has a Story

THE MODERN BIRTH EXPERIENCE is probably the best example of how we've allowed the mystique of technology to subjugate women's intuition and inborn abilities. Throughout history, women gave birth at home without outside interference. It was viewed as a natural life event, not a medical condition.

You can feel comfortable returning to this approach today by learning the story behind each procedure involved before, during, and after the birth of your baby. As a parent, you'll face numerous routine interventions for your child and will need to decide whether they should be administered, delayed, or even refused. Parents are often not aware that many of the standardized recommendations about how to care for babies and children are not grounded in evidence-based practice.

Also, the concept of informed consent—which involves the consent of the patient—becomes a tremendous ethical issue when it relates to performing procedures or administering medication to your child. Infants and children cannot be their own advocates. They can't be adequately informed about procedures and medications nor are they capable of understanding their ramifications. In these situations, you are the advocate, and the informed permission of you the

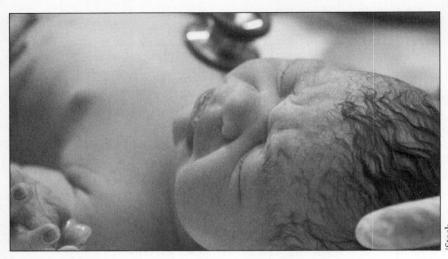

iStock

Several procedures have become standard for newborns, but not all of them are necessary. For example, if newborns are put to the breast soon after birth, the injection of vitamin K is not required because the colostrums or "first milk" that comes from the mother's breast immediately following delivery and for about the first four days is usually rich in nutrients, including vitamin K.

parent substitutes for the decision-making capability, or lack thereof, of your child. As such, the legal and moral authority to accept or refuse treatment falls to you.

The Beginning: The Birth of Your Newborn

After a baby is born, there are several procedures that have become "routine" aspects of post-natal care. You might find yourself becoming frustrated with all of the conflicting information about standardized care for newborns. As with routine medical intervention during birth, it can be valuable to consider these practices as options rather than requirements and to do some research as to the benefits and drawbacks of each.

While the health of your newborn should be the determining factor in how your baby is handled, standard newborn care varies tremendously depending on where the birth occurs. You may want to look into the differences in customary procedures among hospitals, birth centers, and home births in your area.

Rooming In

Throughout most of human history, mothers and babies have stayed together after birth. While hospitals had strayed from this concept over the years, keeping mother and child together has once again has become part of the normal birth routine in many hospitals, largely due to the combined efforts of La Leche League and other childbirth activists, including pediatricians Marshall Klaus and John Kennell. In *Parent-Infant Bonding*, first published in 1976, Klaus and Kennell point out the existence of a "sensitive period" of bonding immediately after birth, during which maternal-infant attachment seems to occur more readily than if mother and child are separated.

One way you can better connect with your baby is by giving birth in an environment that allows you to be with your baby all the time. "Bonding" in this context does not mean just a few short minutes before the baby is taken to the nursery to be washed, weighed, wrapped, and warmed. *There is absolutely no reason why a healthy baby should be separated from you. Mothers who give birth in a hospital can request that all newborn procedures occur at their bedside.* These procedures include weighing, measuring, administering eye ointment, the newborn exam, heel stick blood test (used to screen for rare genetic metabolic diseases), vitamin K injection, and bathing, if desired.

When your baby is bathed in the nursery he can lose much of his body heat and have a hard time maintaining his temperature. And if your baby is then placed in a warming bassinet, that can further exacerbate the separation from you. Ideally, your baby should be warmed by being placed next to you, with a blanket over both of you.

In most human societies, infants are not placed in a separate room away from their mothers for prolonged periods. The baby has a need to feel safe and secure through close human contact. Though policies are slow to change, one result of recent attachment-parenting awareness has been that "rooming in" has become popular in many hospitals. By remaining close, parents can read and respond to their baby's cues, and when they sense that their baby wants something, they can meet that need quickly.

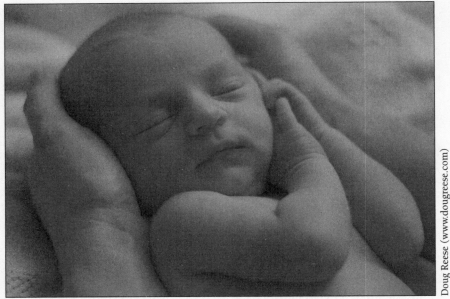

Babies need to feel safe and secure by being touched and held physically. The natural bonding process between newborn and mother helps the baby build up immunity to diseases.

Beyond the bathing issue, there are other disadvantages of the nursery environment, such as bright lights, noise, infectious viruses and bacteria, and the possibility that your baby might be bottle-fed with sugar water to quiet his crying. The interruption in bonding can even increase the risks of post-partum depression and breast-feeding failure. A newborn staying close to his mother establishes healthy intestinal bacteria in the baby's body, an important base for immunity in months to come.

At no time should the baby be left in the nursery without a parent or family member watching. If you want your baby to receive only breast milk, you should personally see to it that no supplementary bottles with sugar water or formula are given. Once your baby's in the nursery and out of your sight, it's quite common for your wishes to be ignored.

Newborn Vitamin K Injection

The American Academy of Pediatrics recommends that vitamin K be given to all newborns as a single, intramuscular injection. This procedure is controversial in other countries, yet it's almost universal in the United States.

The rationale for vitamin K injection at birth is that all babies are born with a naturally low level of vitamin K, a substance that, by enhancing the blood's clotting ability, is responsible for preventing hemorrhage. A vitamin K "deficiency" can make newborns more susceptible to hemorrhage until the vitamin is manufactured in their systems after the first several days after birth. In a small percentage of newborns, the lack of vitamin K can lead to a cerebral hemorrhage, which has in turn resulted in the universal practice of giving newborns the injection. The risk is quite small, but it does exist; this bleeding occurs in approximately 1 in 10,000 babies.

If newborns are put to the breast soon after birth, the injection of vitamin K is less necessary because the colostrum or "first milk" that comes from the mother's breast immediately and for about the first four days is usually rich in nutrients, among them vitamin K. Therefore, an infant who is breast-fed at birth will receive a natural source of vitamin K, gradually raising the level of the vitamin in the infant's body. Furthermore, while breast milk contains vitamin K, it also contains substances that help the baby build up a healthy amount of digestive bacteria that allows the child to start producing his own vitamin K. Availability and content of vitamin K are greater in the hind milk (the milk that the baby obtains at the end of a breast-feeding) because of its higher fat content, so to receive the full complement of vitamin K in breast milk, the baby needs to completely finish on one breast before being offered the other.

Any practice that involves restricting either the baby's time at the breast or the number of feedings will not allow the baby to receive optimum amounts of vitamin K and will also prolong the time it takes for the baby's intestine to be colonized by friendly, vitamin K-manufacturing bacteria.

ARE BABIES REALLY BORN
WITH A VITAMIN K DEFICIENCY?

The natural sequence of events leading to a successful birth are so highly evolved that it seems unlikely that newborns can accurately be labeled "deficient" in vitamin K. Humanity has survived this far despite the absence of vitamin K being administered at birth. One might wonder if hemorrhagic disease of the newborn is caused less by a deficiency of vitamin K than by the medical procedures before and during the birth. For instance, babies said to be having this bleeding problem were given this diagnosis because they showed prolonged and excessive bleeding following circumcision or blood draws, which are not usually necessary procedures in the early newborn period. The blood level of vitamin K usually rises above adult levels around day seven.

Although oral administration of vitamin K may be an alternative in cases where parents refuse painful intramuscular administration, the oral formulation is not reliably absorbed and several doses are needed over several weeks. As well, there is no licensed oral product, meaning that babies receive the intramuscular form orally, and the preparation has a bitter taste. Babies are inclined to spit it out.

The risk of hemorrhage in newborns can be increased by premature clamping of the umbilical cord, which deprives babies of up to 40 percent of their natural blood volume, including platelets and other clotting factors. Also, under conditions of difficult or traumatic labor, where the use of forceps or vacuum extraction often causes bruising or internal bleeding, the baby's available clotting factors can be used up.

Birth is a time of sensory bombardment for the baby—suddenly being exposed to handling, cold, harsh lights, and the sound of its own cries. The pain that the newborn feels at this juncture by being given an intramuscular injection must be jarring and extremely unpleasant.

If you decide not to give your baby the vitamin K injection, you do need to watch closely for signs of bleeding; and if your child does bleed or show signs of bruising he should be checked by a doctor. Key is that you know you have a choice about this shot. Examine each circumstance carefully. If your newborn is going to be undergoing any procedures that cause bleeding, then you may consider the administration of vitamin K a good precaution as the injection aids in blood clotting. Furthermore, if the birth was traumatic or there is any chance of internal bleeding, vitamin K is an appropriate choice in this circumstance, too. But with a normal birth and a healthy newborn, severe blood loss is an unlikely risk and the vitamin K present in colostrum likely will be sufficient.

> *Birth is a time of sensory bombardment for the baby—suddenly being exposed to handling, cold, harsh lights, and the sound of its own cries. The pain that the newborn feels at this juncture by being given an intramuscular injection must be jarring and extremely unpleasant.*

Newborn Jaundice

Of all the topics connected with newborns, jaundice remains one of the most confusing and misunderstood. It's also an issue that has long made doctors anxious: historically, doctors have over-treated jaundice because recommendations in textbooks were based on the risks to much more sickly babies. If a jaundiced baby was not treated aggressively and something went wrong, doctors worried that they'd get the blame.

In the vast majority of healthy full-term babies, mild newborn jaundice is normal and harmless. Here are the points to consider:

- Jaundice is a common condition in newborns. It is caused by an accumulation of a yellow pigment called *bilirubin* in the body.
- Infants are born with more red blood cells than they need for life outside of the womb. Once the baby starts breathing on his own, his oxygen levels increase, resulting in the rapid destruction of unneeded red blood cells. When the baby breaks down many of these cells in a short amount of time, his body becomes loaded with bilirubin, a by-product of this breakdown (similar to a bruise on a child's knee turning yellow during the healing process). Normally, the liver processes bilirubin so that it can be removed from the body in the stool. However, a newborn's liver is still immature, which can cause the yellow pigment in bilirubin to amass and deposit in the baby's skin. As a result, it is not unusual for a baby's skin to appear slightly yellow. This is considered normal *physiologic jaundice* because it is part of a normal maturing process.
- Physiologic jaundice appears within the first 48 hours after birth, peaks around the third or fourth day, and accounts for the greatest numbers of jaundiced babies.
- Medical professionals have been reluctant to view newborn jaundice as normal. However, elevated bilirubin levels and prolonged jaundice in otherwise healthy breast-fed babies are just normal variants of ordinary physiologic newborn jaundice.

Jaundice and Breast-fed Babies?

You may have heard that jaundice is more common in babies who are breast-fed. Why is this?

The jaundice associated with breast-feeding in the neonatal period has been called "breast milk jaundice" but should more accurately be called "lack of breast milk jaundice." This is because, in the first week, it is not the breast milk that is causing jaundice in babies who are nursing, but infrequent or inefficient feeding that allows a little extra buildup of bilirubin to occur. While a mother's milk is not expected to be fully present for the first three or four days, frequent feedings are still important. Babies who are jaundiced

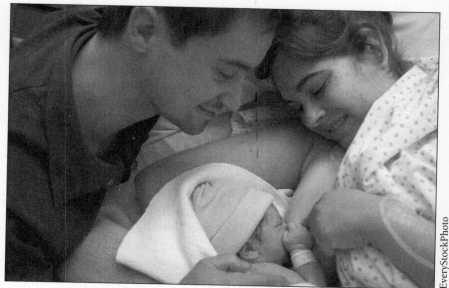

EveryStockPhoto

Newborns should not have formula. They need a mother's nutrient-rich milk. Breastfeeding helps eliminate bilirubin from your baby's body. A baby with jaundice needs to be breast-fed frequently. Choose a birthing environment that allows you to give your baby only breast milk.

need to be breast-fed more, not less. Any supplements of artificial formula feeding interfere with this process, and discourages breast-feeding at this most important time.

Jaundice is not caused by a mother's milk. Early, frequent, unrestricted breast-feeding helps to eliminate bilirubin from your baby's body. Further, feedings do not need to be lengthy to be effective. Mothers can help by nursing the baby ten to twelve times every twenty-four hours. Bilirubin exits the body in the infant's stool, and because breast milk has a laxative effect, babies who

> *Jaundice is not caused by a mother's milk. Babies who are jaundiced need to be breast-fed more, not less. Early, frequent, unrestricted breast-feeding helps to eliminate bilirubin from your baby's body.*

breast-feed frequently tend to have a lot of soiled diapers and thus lower bilirubin levels. If babies don't take in enough milk, they won't have bowel movements, and if they don't have bowel movements, their bodies won't eliminate bilirubin. Mother's milk will usually "come in" within a day or two after jaundice is diagnosed. Establishing good breast-feeding habits before this time will help with good milk intake once the breasts are fully producing milk.

Problems arise when the infant is poorly latched-on or fed at infrequent intervals. As babies become more jaundiced, they might become sleepy and nurse less enthusiastically, so they can become dehydrated. You may have to take the lead and wake your baby during the day or night to encourage nursing.

As long as your baby is otherwise healthy, jaundice is usually short-lived and harmless. Common medical interventions for jaundice can interfere with getting breast-feeding off to a good start, so parents and healthcare providers need to be cautious about jaundice cures that can create more problems than the disease.

Many pediatricians still lack strong foundations in breast-feeding and are more familiar with formula-fed newborns that have slightly lower bilirubin levels. It is not uncommon for doctors to recommend that a mother temporarily discontinue breast-feeding and give babies bottles of supplementary solutions to reduce bilirubin levels. This has been shown to be ineffective and may even increase your baby's jaundice by interfering with the natural physiologic processes of the breakdown and excretion of bilirubin.

Complementary formula feeds and water supplementation can additionally aggravate the jaundice by creating confusion for your baby about feeding methods. Babies who are given glucose solutions or artificial formula nurse less vigorously and less often, thus decreasing colostrum and breast milk intake, as well as causing breast engorgement for the mother. As mentioned, reduced milk intake results in less bilirubin excreted in stools. Researchers have consistently noted an increase in bilirubin levels with the routine use of glucose water after nursings.

Bilirubin Lights

Doctors sometimes recommend special bilirubin lights when the baby is showing signs of jaundice.

If bilirubin levels are slightly elevated, your baby usually doesn't require any "treatment" other than increasing the frequency of breast-feeding, which will aid in eliminating the bilirubin.

In some situations, however, jaundice may be the result of problems beyond the normal breakdown of excessive red blood cells. Abnormally high bilirubin levels can result from premature birth, stress from a difficult birth, a diabetic mother, or blood-type incompatibility between mother and baby. In these situations, if the pediatrician suspects that something more than normal physiologic jaundice is the cause of the baby's yellow color, bilirubin levels should be monitored more closely. If levels are high or increasing rapidly, the doctor may recommend light therapy (also referred to as bili lights or phototherapy). Phototherapy helps break down bilirubin in the baby's skin. It is traditionally done in the hospital for one to two days, during which time the baby is placed naked under specific lights. The baby's eyes are covered for protection.

Phototherapy

Phototherapy is generally considered safe and relatively harmless, but the treatment often needlessly alarms parents and can interfere with the earliest stages of breast-feeding and other steps in developing the mother-child bond.

If phototherapy treatment is necessary because of a high bilirubin level, talk to your doctor about alternatives to placing your baby in the hospital nursery under phototherapy lights. Some babies can be treated at the hospital on an out-patient basis, which is far better than having them admitted.

Home treatment can be an even better option. For most babies a photo-optic bilirubin-blanket (phototherapy lights that wrap around the baby) works well. You can hold and breast-feed your baby at home while the lights dissolve the bilirubin. When it's the right time of year, a little healthy sunshine often will reduce the bilirubin sufficiently. (Babies kept in darkened rooms for the first few days tend to have higher bilirubin levels than those liberally exposed to sunlight.)

When an infant does require treatment, the mother should continue nursing and offering frequent feedings. While jaundiced babies can sometimes be sleepy, phototherapy often makes them more so, and even less interested in feeding, so you may find it takes a little extra effort to wake them up.

Aggressive management styles and misinformation from other parents have caused some parents to believe that jaundice is in itself a terrible illness, that it indicates that their baby is generally unhealthy, or in grave danger. This is simply not the case. In fact, more dangerous is what has been called "vulnerable child syndrome," in which parents of healthy-but-jaundiced babies are more likely than mothers of babies who were not jaundiced to think of their children as vulnerable to illness for years after the birth. In most cases, parents can be assured that the infant is healthy and that the jaundice is a transitional event.

Initiating Breast-feeding

The Centers for Disease Control and Prevention (CDC) has issued a report[1] saying that U.S. hospitals and birth centers should improve breast-feeding support.

Nearly 2,700 hospitals and birthing centers were surveyed about maternity practices and evaluated on a 100-point scale for procedures during the intrapartum period. These practices included:

- Ensuring mother-newborn skin-to-skin contact
- Keeping mother and newborn together
- Not giving supplemental feedings to breast-fed newborns unless medically indicated
- Breast-feeding support after discharge

THE TEN STEPS TO SUCCESSFUL BREAST-FEEDING:

- Have a written breast-feeding policy that is routinely communicated to all healthcare staff.
- Train all healthcare staff in skills necessary to implement this policy.
- Inform all pregnant women about the benefits and management of breast-feeding.
- *Help mothers initiate breast-feeding within an hour of birth.
- Show mothers how to breast-feed and how to maintain lactation, even if they should be separated from their infants.
- *Give newborn infants no food or drink other than breast milk, unless medically indicated.
- *Practice "rooming in" by allowing mothers and infants to remain together twenty-four hours a day.
- Encourage breast-feeding on demand.
- *Give no artificial nipples, pacifiers, dummies, or soothers to breast-feeding infants.
- *Foster the establishment of breast-feeding support groups and refer mothers to them on discharge from the hospital or birthing center.

> * Implementing these five breast-feeding-friendly practices in hospitals following birth can significantly improve long-term breast-feeding success, according to a 2007 study in *Birth: Issues in Perinatal Care.*

The findings indicate a substantially high presence of maternity practices that are not evidence-based and are known to interfere with breast-feeding. For example, 24 percent of birth facilities reported supplementing more than half of healthy, full-term, breast-fed newborns with something other than breast milk during the postpartum stay, a practice shown to be unnecessary and detrimental to breast-feeding. In addition, 70 percent of facilities reported giving breast-feeding mothers gift bags containing infant formula samples.

The report states that facilities should consider discontinuing these practices to provide more positive influences on both breast-feeding initiation and duration. Research has indicated that the more that supportive breast-feeding practices are in place, the stronger the positive effect will be on breast-feeding.

Also, the facilities that give breast-feeding mothers infant-formula discharge packs should consider discontinuing these practices in order to provide more positive influences regarding breast-feeding.

(Birth centers in the CDC study had higher mean total scores in breast-feeding support, compared with hospitals. Scores were highest in Vermont, New Hampshire, Rhode Island, Maine, Alaska, Montana, Oregon, and Washington. The lowest scores were in Arkansas, Mississippi, and Louisiana.)

The Baby-Friendly Hospital Initiative (BFHI) is an international program of the World Health Organization (WHO) and the United Nations Children's Fund (UNICEF). The Initiative acknowledges hospitals and birth centers that have put in place policies and practices to enable parents to make informed choices about how they feed and care for their babies. Baby-Friendly birth facilities have taken special steps to create the best possible environment for successful breast-feeding. Birthing facilities implementing the Ten Steps (see sidebar on page 21) create an optimal environment for the initiation of breast-feeding.[3]

The most natural initiation of breast-feeding is in the first minutes to first hours after birth, with skin-to-skin contact. During this time, most infants are alert and interested in nursing. This helps mothers and infants to achieve optimal breast-feeding.

Benefits of Colostrum

Having the baby room-in with the mother helps to assure that breast-feeding gets off to a good start and that the baby receives colostrum, which is rich in nutrients and calories and typically supplies everything your baby will need during the first few days.

Colostrum has many important properties:

- It is extremely easy to digest, and is therefore the perfect first food for your baby. It is highly concentrated nutrition for the newborn.
- Colostrum coats the lining of the intestines, which helps prevent foreign substances from passing through the intestinal walls into the blood stream. This makes it more difficult for micro-organisms and allergens to get into the baby's body.
- Colostrum stimulates the baby to have bowel movements, so that meconium (the first stool) is cleared quickly from the gut. This also helps get rid of the bilirubin that produces jaundice in the baby's body.
- Colostrum has a high concentration of immune factors and acts as a natural vaccine.

Because your body will only produce a small amount of colostrum immediately after delivery, you may worry that your baby isn't getting enough to eat. However, infants are born with an excess of fluid and sugar stores, which they are able to use as your milk supply gradually increases.

BANNING FORMULA

An increasing number of hospitals across the United States, in an effort to promote breast-feeding, are banning free gift bags that contain samples of infant formula, which often are given to women when they leave the hospital after delivery.

Mothers who take home a formula company gift bag are more likely to stop exclusively breast-feeding their babies by ten weeks of age, according to a 2008 study[2] in the American Journal of Public Health.

Among those women in the study who were breast-feeding when they left the hospital, more than two-thirds said they had received hospital discharge formula packs.

When hospitals give out free formula, it is an implicit endorsement of artificial feeding. This practice has the effect of discouraging exclusive and prolonged breast-feeding.

The researchers conclude that "Commercial hospital discharge packs are one of several factors that influence breast-feeding duration and exclusivity. The distribution of these packs to new mothers at hospitals is part of a longstanding marketing campaign by infant formula manufacturers and implies hospital and staff endorsement of infant formula. Commercial hospital discharge pack distribution should be reconsidered in light of its negative impact on exclusive breast-feeding."

"Hospitals shouldn't be giving out discharge gift packs to new mothers," recommended Dr. Kenneth Rosenberg, chief author of the study.

Don't worry... it's normal to produce only small amounts of this first milk in the beginning. With continued, frequent breast-feeding, a larger amount of mature milk will be produced within two or three days. Infants normally lose weight during the first few days and gradually regain this weight by two weeks after delivery.

Do not give your baby supplemental formula. Artificial feeding reduces the demand for a mother's milk. This can quickly create a downward spiral of supply and demand. Sometimes the mother thinks she doesn't have enough milk and, by using formula, this can come true.

Lactoferrin

Lactoferrin (*lacto*=milk, *ferrin*=iron), found in high concentrations in human milk and colostrum, is a protein that binds to iron. It is a natural substance that promotes the growth of healthy bacteria in the intestine, and inhibits the growth of disease-causing bacteria such as E. coli, streptococcus, clostridium, and staphylococci. Lactoferrin is not available in formulas.

The amount of lactoferrin in breast milk gradually decreases after the first few days, but then persists in the milk throughout lactation. When infants are breast-fed, lactoferrin brings about a dramatic increase in "good" micro-organisms in the intestine—such as bifidus—and keeps "bad" bacteria to a minimum. The result is a desirable level of beneficial intestinal bacteria, which is known to be essential for optimal health, immunity, and resistance to disease. One bottle of formula is all it takes to alter the establishment of this healthy bacteria.

> *When infants are breast-fed, lactoferrin brings about a dramatic increase in "good" micro-organisms in the intestine —such as bifidus— and keeps "bad" bacteria to a minimum. One bottle of formula is all it takes to alter the establishment of this healthy bacteria.*

PKU Test

State laws require that babies receive a heel-stick blood test to screen for a number of rare genetic metabolic diseases, including *phenylketonuria* (PKU). The baby's blood is smeared onto an absorbent paper on the second day after birth, usually before leaving the hospital. PKU prevents the baby from processing phenylalanine, an amino acid. Babies with this disorder will experience brain damage unless they are put on a special diet soon after birth. However, for results to be most accurate, babies should be breast-fed for several days before taking the test. You can sign a waiver and then take the baby to the pediatrician to receive the test later. Because these disorders are rare, many homebirth parents decide to either forgo the procedure or wait a week until breast-feeding is established before having the baby tested.

Circumcision

There are a myriad of reasons why parents either choose or forgo circumcision. The procedure has its staunch advocates and its fierce opponents, and it is beyond the scope of this book to present all of the research available on the benefits and drawbacks.

Opponents of circumcision argue that it's a painful procedure that is unethical and unnecessary because it does not treat any disease, injury, or other health problem. In the United States, circumcision has always been common, although it became less so after the mid-1970s, when the view that it was against nature gained ground. Circumcision seems to be on the rise again following recent reports in the literature citing various health benefits.[5]

Still, most parents who choose circumcision for their sons do it for non-medical reasons, based on concerns about hygiene, religious beliefs, or cultural or social reasons. Ease of cleanliness is the most common reason that parents choose circumcision. Approximately 60 percent of male babies in the United States today are circumcised. If you're considering circumcision for your son, you have the options of requesting that pain medication be administered and of having a parent present at the procedure. When the circumcision is done as part of a Jewish ritual religious ceremony, it is done on the eighth day, and as such avoids the period of low levels of natural vitamin K.

Hepatitis B Vaccine

Hepatitis B vaccine is offered in the days after birth as a standard practice but may not be the right choice for every family. Parents will want to become familiar with this vaccine before their baby is born so that they can make their wishes known. Other vaccinations are covered in a later chapter.

Hepatitis B is an illness caused by a blood-borne virus that attacks the liver. Unlike other infectious diseases for which vaccines have been developed and mandated in the United States, hepatitis B is not common in childhood and it is not highly contagious. It is not fatal for most that contract it. For those who acquire the disease naturally, a great percentage of patients have a favorable course, recover completely, and acquire lifelong immunity.

The vast majority of newborns are not at risk of contracting hepatitis B, which is primarily an adult disease transmitted through infected body fluids, most frequently infected blood. It is often contracted by needle-using drug addicts who share drug paraphernalia, sexually promiscuous heterosexual and homosexual adults, those who receive tattoos, residents and staff of custodial institutions such as prisons, and healthcare workers accidentally exposed to contaminated blood. It can also be transmitted from an infected mother to a baby during birth, which is virtually the only risk factor for a newborn. Those infants at risk due to maternal infection are identified by prenatal screening.

In 1991, the Centers for Disease Control and Prevention (CDC) recommended that all infants receive their first dose of the hepatitis B vaccine at birth before being discharged from the hospital despite the fact that newborns have minimal chance for infection; therefore the vaccine is of no benefit to the infant at that time and it likely never will be.

As with other vaccines, the duration of the protective effect conferred by the hepatitis B vaccine is artificial and temporary. Therefore, the vaccine is given three separate times to infants over the first few months. Future need for more "booster" doses later in life is unknown.

Many parents are unaware that they have a choice about this vaccination. Some parents choose to delay the hepatitis B vaccine while others forgo this vaccine altogether.

Eye Treatment

The application of silver nitrate or an antibiotic ointment such as tetracycline or erythromycin into the eyes of newborn babies just minutes after birth is another routine procedure in the United States. This is called eye *prophylaxis*. The word "prophylaxis" means prevention or protection from disease. Eye prophylaxis is recommended by the American Academy of Pediatrics and the CDC, and is mandated by law in all fifty states.

In most cases, the eye treatment is not needed because the mother is known to be free from infection through screening for sexually transmitted diseases (STDs), which is now a standard part of prenatal care.

This procedure was originally required to prevent blindness from exposure of the infant to maternal gonorrhea during birth, because women with gonorrhea infections can possibly pass the infection to their baby during passage through the birth canal. To prevent the infection, public health law dictates that every baby receive this eye treatment (including babies born by cesarean). In most cases, the eye treatment is not needed because the mother is known to be free from infection through screening for sexually transmitted diseases (STDs), which is now a standard part of prenatal care.

Shutter Stock

Eye prophylaxis can cause some stinging, irritation, itching, redness, sensitivity to light, and temporarily blurred vision in a newborn that can interfere with a baby's ability to bond with his mother. In most cases, the eye treatment is not needed because the mother is known to be free from infection through screening for sexually transmitted diseases (STDs), which is now a standard part of prenatal care.

In the 1970s, silver nitrate was the only available eye prophylaxis for newborn babies to prevent the development of blindness if the mother had gonorrhea. It is still used on occasion today, although antibiotic ointments are more common. The silver nitrate bonds with the eye membranes, which results in redness, blurred vision, and swelling for several days. This interferes with bonding, visual perception, and adjustment to the new environment outside of the womb.

When many parents refused silver nitrate because of these effects, erythromycin antibiotic ointment became the eye prophylaxis of choice. Information on the erythromycin ointment—which most facilities use—says that serious side effects are not expected, but that some stinging, irritation, itching, redness, blurred vision (lasting about thirty minutes), or sensitivity to light may occur.

According to medical research studies, there is no clear benefit to this routinely applied ointment compared with not giving any ointment or drops at all.[6] Also, there is evidence that the bacteria that

IS EYE TREATMENT NECESSARY
IF YOU DON'T HAVE GONORRHEA?

Prophylactic eye treatment of the newborn is based on the un-supported idea that the mother and her newborn have a disease or deficiency that needs to be cured or prevented by society's medical intervention. If you are concerned about this proce-dure, you can choose to delay its administration to allow bond-ing time between you and your new baby, preventing discomfort from being one of the child's earliest sensory experiences. Depending on the laws of your community, you may be able to delay this treatment for two hours, or exercise your rights re-garding freedom of choice in your baby's healthcare and refuse the procedure if you know that you don't have an STD.

---

cause these infections are not passed to the infant in the birth canal, but after birth. Finally, while some doctors recommend the eye oint-ment to prevent conjunctivitis from other organisms (such as one called chlamydia), it has been found that a significant number of in-fants develop an infection even after having received the ointment. [7]

Now you know . . .

Standard medical procedures have transformed what is a natural life event into a series of interventions that are potentially harmful to your baby. And while you may elect to go through with some of these procedures, not every event in your child's early life is a problem to be solved. You know that at every juncture, you have a choice. Trust your instincts, and trust that you know what's best for your child.

Footnotes

1. www.cdc.gov/mmwr/preview/mmwrhtml/mm5723a1.htm.
2. www.ajph.org/cgi/content/abstract/98/2/290.
3. www.cdphe.state.co.us/release/2007/082407.html.
4. In evaluating the benefits of breast milk, the American Academy of Pediatrics conducted a review of the literature for evidence of disease reduction with the use of human milk. In their policy statement on breast-feeding, they found "strong evidence" that breast milk reduces the incidence and/or severity of diseases such as diarrhea, lower respiratory infections, ear infections, bacterial meningitis, and urinary tract infections. (American Academy of Pediatrics Work Group on Breast-feeding, *Pediatrics*, 1997, Vol. 100, 1035–1039)].
5. Arch Pediatr Adolesc Med., 2010, Vol. 164, 78–84, 94–96.
6. Chen, J. Y., "Prophylaxis of ophthalmia neonatorum: comparison of silver nitrate, tetracycline, erythromycin and no prophylaxis," *Pediatr Infect Dis J*, December 1992 Vol. 11, Issue 12, 1026–1030.
7. Black-Payne, C., J. A. Bocchini, Jr., and C. Cedotal, "Failure of erythromycin ointment for postnatal ocular prophylaxis of chlamydial conjunctivitis," *Pediatr Infect Dis J*, August 1989, Vol. 8, Issue 8, 491–495.

Charlotte Yonge

2

Breast-feeding

FOR MOST OF HUMAN EXISTENCE, mothers have fed their babies breast milk. As discussed in the first chapter, breast-feeding is one of the amazing abilities given to women as a natural part of the life cycle, and the many benefits of breast-feeding are well known. As more mothers are encouraged to trust their own instincts over industry-driven advice, they are coming to understand and enjoy their unique ability to provide superior nutrition along with the emotional attachment that comes with nursing a baby.

Each mammal species makes milk that is uniquely suited for its young. Are you aware that cow's milk is the basis of most commercial infant formulas? Yet cow's milk is biologically specific for baby cows, not human babies. So why give this to your baby? Would you give an infant horse milk or dog milk?

Your breast milk is the best for your baby—that is to say, perfect. It provides all of the nutrients he needs for at least the first six months. But evidence points to the fact that breast milk goes beyond nourishment and may well take on the characteristics of a medicine or vaccine. In fact, the U.S. Transportation Security Administration puts breast milk in the same category as "liquid medications."[1]

Let's be very clear about one thing: the breast milk recipe isn't just hard to beat—it's impossible.

Breast milk has so many ingredients, which give it so many necessary biological properties for maintaining health and promoting proper growth and development. The milk's unique enzymes, hormones, antibodies, and immunoglobulins simply can't be recreated commercially, although that hasn't stopped formula manufacturers from trying.

> *Let's be very clear about one thing: the breast milk recipe isn't just hard to beat— it's impossible.*

Formula makers spend billions on fancy marketing geared toward convincing you that their brand is the "most like mother's milk," while agreeing that breast milk is best. It even says so right on the label.

More Than a "Parenting Choice"

For so long, whether or not to breast-feed has been couched as a "parenting choice," a message reinforced by those formula company slogans. Far from being simply a lifestyle preference, breast-feeding is a major public health issue with far-reaching medical and economic benefits.

For instance, a study that was published in the journal *Pediatrics* in April 2010 brings home the point that artificial feeding of infants places a tremendous economic and health burden on our society. The research showed that if most new mothers give only breast milk to their babies for the first six months, it would save many infant lives and avoid many more costly illnesses each year from health problems that breast-feeding can help prevent.

The illnesses for which breast-feeding is known to be protective (as delineated by the U.S. government's Agency for Healthcare Research and Quality) include necrotizing enterocolitis, otitis media, gastroenteritis, lower respiratory tract infections requiring hospitalization, atopic dermatitis, sudden infant death syndrome, childhood asthma, childhood leukemia, type 1 diabetes mellitus, and childhood obesity.

Your breast milk is the best for your baby—that is to say, perfect. And far from being simply a lifestyle preference, breast-feeding is a major public health issue with far-reaching medical and economic benefits.

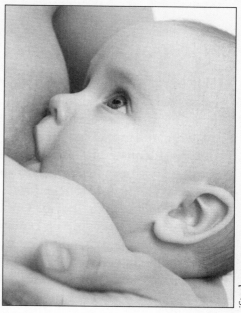

iStock

Researchers evaluated the costs of treating these diseases and concluded that if 90 percent of all American mothers chose to breast-feed exclusively in the first six months, *$13 billion per year could be saved*—all while saving lives and avoiding illness.[2]

Exclusive breast-feeding means no other nutritional source, including water, infant food, juice, formula, cow's milk (never recommended for infants anyway) or "sugar water." Considering that many fortunate babies (and mothers) continue to benefit from breast-feeding even well beyond six months, the results of the study, compelling as they are, could even be considered conservative.

Brain Development in Breast-feeding vs. Artificial Feeding

Cow's milk, which as stated earlier forms the foundation for most commercial infant formulas, is high in protein and minerals, which baby calves need for rapid muscle and bone growth. If human babies were fed only pure cow's milk, they simply would not survive. Human milk, by contrast, is high in nutrients that promote brain growth; children who were breast-fed tend to score higher on intelligence quotient (IQ) tests. Several studies have demonstrated that babies who are exclusively breast-fed for at least the first three months and, sometimes, for the first year, have better cognitive abilities and

HEALTH AGENCY RECOMMENDATIONS

The World Health Organization (WHO) says infants should be exclusively breast-fed for the first six months "to achieve optimal growth, development and health...Thereafter, to meet their evolving nutritional requirements, infants should receive nutritionally adequate and safe complementary foods while breast-feeding continues for up to two years of age or beyond."[3]

The WHO is not alone in its recommendations:

The American College of Obstetricians and Gynecologists, the American Academy of Pediatrics, the American Academy of Family Physicians, and the Centers for Disease Control and Prevention all agree that breast milk alone is sufficient for newborns and infants until they are six months old.

The Agency for Healthcare Research and Quality is the lead federal agency charged with improving the quality, safety, efficiency, and effectiveness of healthcare for all Americans. This Department of Health and Human Services agency has reported the following illnesses as preventable by breast-feeding: necrotizing enterocolitis, otitis media, gastroenteritis, hospitalization for lower respiratory tract infections, atopic dermatitis, sudden infant death syndrome, childhood asthma, childhood leukemia, type 1 diabetes mellitus, and childhood obesity.[4]

---

general intelligence as they grow than children who were formula fed. For instance, compared with children who were fed formula early on, breast-fed babies registered far higher scores for verbal IQ, performance IQ, and general IQ when they were tested at the age of six-and-a-half. Researchers made the discovery when they assessed the cognitive development of 13,889 children who were exclusively breast-fed for a prolonged period.[5]

Another study in December 2009 showed that breast-feeding promotes development of white matter in the brain (the tissue through which messages pass between different areas of the nervous system), therefore providing evidence that the increased cognitive development of breast-fed infants is not simply linked to economic or educational factors involved in a mother's decision to breast-feed.[6]

Yet another study showed that longer-duration breast-feeding was associated with improved infant development, particularly at 18 months; babies were more advanced in reaching such milestones as climbing stairs, removing their socks, drinking from a cup, writing or drawing, using word-like sounds and putting words together, and walking unassisted. This research, conducted by the Harvard Medical School as well as the Statens Serum Institute in Denmark, observed 25,446 children born to women participating in the Danish Birth Cohort Study between 1997 and 2002.[7]

Soy

For various reasons many non-breast-feeding parents see soy-based formula—which utilizes the proteins found in soybeans—as their best option. Some choose soy because they assume it is less allergenic or more likely to curb reflux issues or fussiness in colicky babies—all problems seen in cow-milk fed babies. Others choose soy formula based on concerns that cattle are fed hormones and antibiotics that find their way into their milk, which, as noted earlier, forms the basis of non-soy formulas. Some parents feel that, all other things being apparently equal, soy projects more of a "natural" character that might be in keeping with their own dietary priorities.

- Aside from the fact that a large percentage of infants who have allergic reactions to cow's milk formula also exhibit an allergic response to soy-based formula, there are several other major issues with soy formula that render it an unsafe food for infants. Soybeans are high in phytic acid, which is known to block the body's absorption of such minerals as calcium, zinc, magnesium, and iron, all required for the health and development of the brain and nervous system.

- Soy contains isoflavones, plant hormones that mimic estrogen in the body. Some research has shown that isolated isoflavones, also known as phytoestrogens, contribute to the growth of tumors in the breast, endometrium, and uterus. Also, phytoestrogens in soy formula have been implicated in the current trend toward increasingly premature sexual development in girls and delayed or retarded sexual development in boys.

> *Soybeans are high in phytic acid, which is known to block the body's absorption of such minerals as calcium, zinc, magnesium, and iron, all required for the health and development of the brain and nervous system.*

- Soy lacks cholesterol, an essential nutrient for the development of the brain and nervous system. It is possible that children are less likely to reach their intellectual potential if they do not receive sufficient cholesterol in the first two years of their lives.
- There is continuing concern about very high levels of aluminum in soy formula based on a 1998 study. Soy processing involves acid washing and neutralization solutions in huge industrial tanks that leach aluminum.
- Soy has one of the highest pesticide contamination levels of any crop.
- Soy formula has extremely high levels of manganese, a nutrient that is critical but neurologically harmful at high doses. Soy formula has 80 times the amount of manganese as human breast milk.

Lifestyle

As a practical matter, as long as women are surrounded by adequate support, breast-feeding is easier than bottle-feeding. Breast-feeding is simple and natural. Perhaps it does not always seem that way, because we have lost our gathered wisdom as women and we are not sharing with each other and learning as we grow up. With proper encouragement, virtually all women can breast-feed. Breast milk is convenient and free, always ready, always at the perfect temperature, and doesn't need to be measured. There are no bottles to purchase, clean, and transport, and no formula to buy, keep cooled, and then warmed. Night feedings are easier because all you have to do is tuck the baby in bed with you. Traveling is easier with a nursing baby, as there is much less to carry.

Breast-feeding can be done anywhere, making it easier than bottle-feeding. Breast milk is convenient and free, always ready, always at the perfect temperature.

Immunology

There are immunological consequences to not breast-feeding your baby. Breast milk contains antiviral, antibacterial, antifungal, and antiprotozoal properties as well as antibodies to many specific disease organisms. These factors and antibodies protect your baby against illness.

Breast milk contains natural *probiotics*, substances that promote the growth of protective bacteria—especially *Lactobacillus* and *Bifidobacteria*—in their gastrointestinal tracts,[8] while in formula-fed babies, there are high levels of less desirable *Streptococcus foecalis* and *E. coli*.[9] Breast-fed babies have a lower incidence of many infectious diseases because of the milk's beneficial bacteria.

> *Although the AAP as an organization is cognizant of the many benefits of human milk, many individual pediatricians do not actively encourage the official policy of "breast milk and nothing but" for the first six months.*

The American Academy of Pediatrics (AAP) conducted a review of the literature for evidence that breast milk reduces disease. In their policy statement on breast-feeding, the AAP found "strong evidence" that breast milk reduces the incidence and/or severity of diseases such as diarrhea, lower respiratory infections, ear infections, bacterial meningitis, and urinary tract infections.[10]

Although the AAP as an organization is cognizant of the many benefits of human milk, many individual pediatricians do not actively encourage the official policy of "breast milk and nothing but" for the first six months.

Allergy

For babies that aren't breast-fed, the most common consequence is that they develop an allergy to whatever substance is in the artificial feeding (cow's milk- or soy-based formulas). The absorption of these foreign (nonhuman) proteins through an immature digestive tract into the bloodstream causes early sensitization and development of atopic dermatitis (eczema) and other manifestations of allergy. Giving a breast-fed baby even a single bottle of formula in the nursery can increase the risk of the baby developing an allergy.

Vitamin D

Concerns about vitamin D sufficiency and breast-feeding have been raised by the American Academy of Pediatrics (AAP), which now recommends vitamin D supplementation for all infants and children to ensure that the small percentage of infants/children who need additional vitamin D do not become deficient. In severe cases, when babies don't have enough of the vitamin, they can develop rickets—a condition where the bones become soft and weak. The AAP recommends that exclusively and partially breast-fed infants receive 400 IU/day of supplemental vitamin D shortly after birth and continue to receive these supplements until they are weaned.

This is simply another situation where nature is considered to be "deficient," when it's not the case. Babies rarely need vitamin D supplements. Even though the amount of vitamin D in human milk is small, it's in a form that is very easily used by the baby and therefore adequate for most infants. Any lack of adequate vitamin D is really due to "deficiencies" in modern-day lifestyles, often leading mothers and babies to be deprived of sunlight. Vitamin D is not really a vitamin—it's a hormone produced in the body after exposure to ultraviolet B (UVB) rays. The way that our bodies were designed to get the vast majority of our vitamin D is from modest sun exposure.

Babies are at risk for vitamin D deficiency *only* in situations where they or their mothers lack exposure to sufficient sunlight. This would be due to such things as:

- Indoor confinement during the day
- Living at higher latitudes
- Living in urban areas with tall buildings and pollution that block sunlight
- Darker skin pigmentation
- Use of sunscreen
- Covering much or all of the body when outside

Going outdoors is generally all that is required for you or your baby to generate adequate amounts of vitamin D. The baby does not need much outside exposure and does not need to go out every day. Vitamin D is a fat-soluble vitamin and is stored in the liver for future use. For babies, only about thirty minutes of exposure each week, wearing just a diaper, is required, while in winter-time a clothed infant not wearing a hat needs only two hours per week of sunshine.[11]

In the summer, when excessive sunlight exposure can cause sunburn and increase the risk of skin cancer, it's safer to be outdoors before 10 A.M. or after 3 P.M.

Iron

The iron in human milk, while small in amount, is extremely well absorbed when an infant is being fed with nothing but breast milk. Such infants have enough iron stores to prevent anemia for six months and well beyond. However, for physiologic reasons, any food or formula that contains iron will actually limit the amount of iron that is available from the breast milk, and accordingly, breast-fed babies are better off without such supplements.

Lactoferrin

Another important issue related to iron is a substance called *lactoferrin,* which was discussed in the first chapter. Lactoferrin is a natural *prebiotic* substance in breast milk that binds to iron. It promotes the growth of healthy bacteria in the intestine, and inhibits the growth of disease-causing bacteria such as *E. coli.* Lactoferrin works because many unhealthy bacteria need a supply of free iron to multiply; in the presence of lactoferrin they are strongly inhibited or killed. If an infant is given formula (or any food containing iron) the lactoferrin in mother's milk is prevented from inhibiting the growth of disease-producing bacteria. Infants are more likely to suffer from infectious diseases, such as ear infections, diarrhea, respiratory infections, and meningitis when receiving any supplemental formula.

IRON SUPPLEMENTS CAN BE HARMFUL

There is actually evidence that iron supplements for infants can be harmful. A ten-year study that was completed in 2008 revealed that the added iron in all formula sold in the United States might be creating developmental delays in infants who are fed such formula.[12]

University of Michigan researchers showed that those infants who received U.S.-made formula, which is highly fortified with iron, lagged behind those who received a low-iron formula like the kind sold in Europe. This involved both cognitive and visual-motor development by age ten.

Manufacturers add iron to formula to prevent iron-deficiency anemia because iron absorption from cow's milk is very low and because formula-fed babies commonly lose iron through intestinal bleeding caused by formula's irritating effects. Iron is needed to make hemoglobin, a substance in red blood cells that enables them to carry oxygen. However, the 5 percent of the infants with the *highest* hemoglobin levels at six months showed the *poorest* outcome in their intelligence and neurological development.

In this randomized study, healthy infants without iron-deficiency anemia were given formula with either 12 milligrams or 2.3 milligrams iron from six to twelve months and followed to ten years. Adversely affected children scored eleven points lower in IQ and twelve points lower in visual-motor integration, on average. When spatial memory and other visual-motor measures were recorded, a similar delay was observed.

SIDS

Breast-feeding has consistently been shown to reduce the risk of sudden infant death syndrome (SIDS). This finding has been noted in several studies in the past decade.

For instance, breast-feeding was shown to reduce the incidence of SIDS by about 50 percent at all ages throughout infancy in a study published in the March 2009 issue of *Pediatrics*, the official journal of the American Academy of Pediatrics. In that research, breast-feeding survival curves showed that both partial breast-feeding and exclusive breast-feeding were associated with a reduced risk of SIDS.[13]

This study, done in Germany, was controlled for such factors as maternal smoking in pregnancy, maternal age at delivery, socioeconomic status, previous live births, infant birth weight, bed sharing in last night, pillow in infant's bed, additional heating in last sleep, sleep position, and pacifier use. The authors of this study link lack of breast-feeding to SIDS:

> This large study...adds to the body of evidence showing that breast-feeding reduces the risk of SIDS, and that this protection continues as long as the infant is breast-fed...The implication of our findings is that these infants would especially benefit from being breast-fed at this early age and that breast-feeding should be continued until the infant is six months of age and the risk of SIDS is low. Breast-feeding is recommended by the World Health Organization on other grounds. The morbidity [illness] and mortality of infants is reduced when they are exclusively breast-fed for the first six months. Being breast-fed also reduces the risk of acute otitis media [ear infections], atopic eczema [rashes], gastrointestinal infections, and lower respiratory infections...Given the weight of evidence...it seems somewhat surprising that breast-feeding has not been included in the American Academy of Pediatrics and United Kingdom Department of Health SIDS prevention recommendations.

> In the last 20 years, the prevention campaigns to reduce the risk of sudden infant death syndrome were very successful...In some countries the advice to breast-feed is included in the campaigns' messages,

but in other countries it is not...We recommend including the advice to breast-feed through six months of age in sudden infant death syndrome risk-reduction messages.

Reduced Breast Cancer Risk

The latest United States research, released in August 2009, suggests that a young mother with a family history of breast cancer can more than halve her risk of getting breast cancer simply by breast-feeding her baby. The findings stem from data on 60,075 nurses who had given birth and who participated in the long-running Nurses' Health Study between 1997 and 2005. Researchers said that these mothers were 59 percent less likely to develop tumors before menopause if they breast-fed their children.[14]

Reduced Cardiovascular Disease

A study released in April 2009 found that women in their 60s who had breast-fed for more than twelve months over the course of their lives were nearly 10 percent less likely to develop cardiovascular disease and significantly less likely to develop heart disease risk factors, such as high blood pressure, diabetes, and high cholesterol.[15]

Oxytocin, Mother's Own Wonder Drug

Nature has provided mothers with a hormone, oxytocin, which connects her emotionally to her baby, helping her to respond to and nurture her infant. Oxytocin is produced during breast-feeding. Levels rise in all women immediately following birth, and continue to rise for weeks in nursing mothers. Among its many benefits, oxytocin:

- Promotes the development of maternal behavior and bonding between mother and her baby
- Is known to create pleasant feelings of wellness

iStock

When a mom breast feeds, her body produces oxytocin, which helps her bond with her baby and creates a feeling of euphoria.

Recent studies have begun to investigate oxytocin's role in various behaviors relating to sociability. It promotes social contact, generosity, and a sense of empathy. Pharmaceutical companies in the United States, Europe, and Asia are trying to capture the benefits of this hormone for profit by supplying it in a commercially available nasal spray form that is promoted as being safe and non-addictive, with no side effects.

"Drug trials" have found that oxytocin can be used to treat a variety of personality disorders such as anxiety, phobias, depression, and autism. As an example, at New York's Mount Sinai School of Medicine, autistic patients were given oxytocin as part of a study. Characteristics of autism include a lack of a sense of empathy toward other people and impairments in social communication and interaction. Deficits in the ability to recognize the emotions of others are believed to contribute to these problems. In this study, those given oxytocin had an increased ability to recognize emotions such as happiness or anger in a person's tone of voice.

A similar study from Australia published in September 2009 provided evidence that oxytocin nasal spray improves emotion recognition in young people diagnosed with autism spectrum disorders, resulting in increased ability to relate to others.[16]

BREAST-FEEDING HELPS MOTHERS

Breast-feeding has numerous health benefits for mothers. Health benefits to a woman who has breast-fed her baby include a reduced risk for:

- Type I and II diabetes
- Anxiety
- Mood disorders
- Osteoporosis
- Breast, ovarian, and uterine cancer
- Depression
- Heart attack, heart disease, and stroke

Environment

Breast milk production does not pollute anything. Unlike artificial methods of feeding, breast-feeding saves world food resources and does not use harmful chemicals in its production. Breast milk is one of the few foodstuffs that is produced and delivered to the consumer without using up any fuel for transportation over long distances from factory to store to home. There is no wasteful packaging. There is no discarded glass, plastic, silicone, or paper using up landfill space. Breast-fed babies are also generally healthier, placing less demand on healthcare services.

Women

Finally, breast-feeding is an important women's issue. Every woman who breast-feeds carries on a tradition of many generations of mothers who have done so successfully and received tremendous satisfaction by seeing their babies grow and thrive in this way.

Now you know . . .

Breast-feeding is the healthiest option for you and your baby. As advocates for children, pediatricians have the responsibility to do everything possible to encourage women to breast-feed, and to ensure that it is a successful and enjoyable experience.

FOOTNOTES

1. U.S. Transportation Security Administration, "Important Information on Traveling With Formula, Breast Milk, and Juice," www.tsa.gov/travelers/airtravel/children/formula.shtm.
2. Melissa Bartick, MD, MSc[a], Arnold Reinhold, MBA, "The Burden of Suboptimal Breast-feeding in the United States: A Pediatric Cost Analysis," *Pediatrics* (doi:10.1542/peds.2009-1616).
3. The World Health Organization's infant feeding recommendation as stated in the *Global Strategy on Infant and Young Child Feeding* (WHA55 A55/15, paragraph 10).
4. "Breast-feeding and Maternal and Infant Health Outcomes in Developed Countries, Agency for Healthcare, Research and Quality," *U.S. Department of Health and Human Services*, April, 2007.
5. Archives of *General Psychiatry*, 2008, Vol. 65, 578–584.
6. "Impact of breast milk on IQ, brain size, and white matter development," *Pediatric Research*, January 5, 2010.
7. *American Journal of Clinical Nutrition*, September 2008, Vol. 88, No. 3, 789–796.
8. *AAP 2000 Red Book: Report of the Committee on Infectious Diseases*, 25th ed. 2000 American Academy of Pediatrics.
9. Gabbe, *Obstetrics—Normal and Problem Pregnancies*, 3rd ed. (Churchill Livingstone, Inc, 1996).
10. American Academy of Pediatrics Work Group on Breast-feeding, *Pediatrics*, 1997, Vol. 100, 035–1039.
11. Specker, et al., "Sunshine exposure and serum 25-hydroxy vitamin D concentrations in exclusively breast-fed infants," *The Journal of Pediatrics*, Vol. 107, Issue 3, 372–376.
12. Betsy Lozoff, Marcela Castillo, and Julia B. Smith, "Poorer developmental outcome at 10 years with 12 mg/L iron-fortified formula in infancy," PAS Meeting 2008; Abstract 5340.2.

13. Vennemann et al., "Does Breast-feeding Reduce the Risk of Sudden Infant Death Syndrome?" *Pediatrics*, March 2009, Vol. 123, Issue 3, e406-e410.

14. Stuebe, et al., "Lactation and Incidence of Premenopausal Breast Cancer, A Longitudinal Study," *Arch Intern Med.*, 2009, Vol. 169, Issue 15, 1364–1371.

15. Schwarz, et al., "Duration of Lactation and Risk Factors for Maternal Cardiovascular Disease, Obstetrics & Gynecology," May 2009, Vol. 113, Issue 5, 974–982.

16. Adam J. Guastella, Ph.D., Brain & Mind Research Institute, University of Sydney, Sydney, NSW 2050, Australia. 2009 Society of Biological Psychiatry. Published by Elsevier Inc.

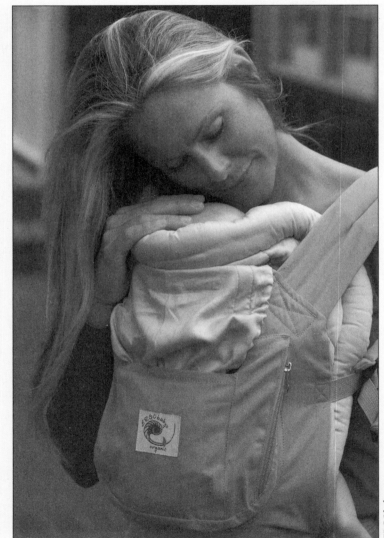

3

Keeping Baby Close: Carrying

"A baby is born with a need to be loved and never outgrows it."
—Frank A. Clark

IN INDUSTRIALIZED WESTERN CULTURES, parents have been conditioned to believe that picking up and holding their baby too much would "spoil" the child and discourage independence. Fortunately, good parental instinct is beginning to win out over a culture that reinforces the big business of baby-containing contraptions, so we are more commonly seeing babies being carried. Our society is rediscovering this instinctive and ancient way of natural parenting and finding it to be enjoyable, ergonomic, practical, and helpful to a baby's physical and social development.

Although carrying a baby in some kind of cloth device may seem like a modern trend, it's a practice that is actually as old as parenting itself. For millennia, parents have worn their babies tied to them with simple wraps or slings to keep the baby close while attending to the normal activities of their daily lives. In many parts of the world, this is still the norm: babies are worn all day, carried, and held until the day they start walking, and beyond.

Holding your baby close mimics the experience of being inside the womb.

Charlotte Yonge

Babies who are held and carried all the time, especially within the first year, are having their need for touch met—and as a result, they will not become clingy and overly dependent. They cry much less[1] and they grow to become happier, more intelligent, more independent, more loving, and more social than babies who spend much of their infancy in infant seats, swings, cribs, and all the other plastic baby-holding devices that don't provide babies with human contact. Meeting a baby's need for touch is just as critical as meeting his need for food and warmth. The physical and psychological benefits associated with close carrying encourage little ones to feel secure and content and build a solid sense of self-esteem.

> Meeting a baby's need for touch is just as critical as meeting his need for food and warmth. The physical and psychological benefits associated with close carrying encourage little ones to feel secure and content and build a solid sense of self-esteem.

The human baby is born the least mature of any mammal. Holding your baby close mimics his experience of being carried inside the womb. The baby is completely enveloped and feels safe and comfortable as he re-experiences the warmth and natural motions. Ashley Montagu, who was an anthropologist, scientist, and humanist, talked about the *eighteen-month gestational period*: nine months within the womb and nine months without or outside of it. The newborn needs that extra nine, even ten months outside of the womb to mature during a period that Dr. Montague designates as *exterogestation*. It's around the end of this period that the infant begins to crawl around and is capable of mobility independent of his mother. The exterogestation period requires the constant care of a loving and nurturing provider who can learn to respond appropriately and quickly to the newborn's needs of touch as well as nourishment and warmth.

Visual Stimulation

Visual stimulation is another benefit of carrying. Unlike a baby on its back (who sees only the ceiling and objects on either side), a baby in a wrap or other carrier will lift his head and view the world at eye level.

Visual stimulation is one of the benefits of carrying. Unlike a baby on its back (who sees only the ceiling and objects on either side), a baby in a wrap or other carrier will lift his head and view the world at eye level.

Girasol

MISSHAPEN HEADS

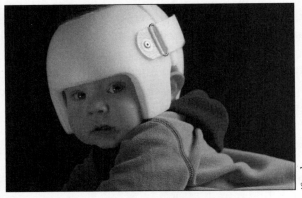

"Back to Sleep" results in misshapen heads.

There has been an alarming increase in skull malformation in recent years because of babies spending so much time on their backs in various cribs and carriers. A number of studies have associated this increase with the 1992 launch of the American Academy of Pediatrics "Back to Sleep" initiative.

For instance, a 2008 study[2] noted that prior to 1992, the prevalence of misshapen heads among infants was reportedly 5 percent. In recent years, craniofacial centers and primary care providers reported a dramatic increase of up to 600 percent in referrals for misshapen heads.

It has also been noticed in recent years that extended use of car seats, infant swings, and bouncy seats is contributing to flat head syndrome, medically known as *plagiocephaly*. In these devices, the back of the head is often against a hard, unyielding surface. While moderate use of these devices is not a concern, extended use, especially to the point of allowing infants to sleep in them, increases plagiocephaly.

If you notice that the back of your baby's head is becoming flat, tell your pediatrician. Once his head becomes flat, it's important to avoid pressure on the flattened areas: as he spends more time lying on his back or reclining with his head on a hard surface such as in a car seat or swing, his skull will be more likely to deform.

Monitor how much time your baby spends in car seats, swings, strollers, and cribs. Car seats should be used only for transporting your infant safely within moving vehicles, and babies should not be left in them to sleep longer than necessary, a problem that's exacerbated when parents use car seats that can be snapped directly into an awaiting stroller setup or swing without having to remove the baby from the seat. This has created a generation of babies who spend prolonged periods of time in one position.

Once your baby is six months old, it's too late to try to change the shape of the head by repositioning. At this point, if your child has developed severe positional plagiocephaly, a doctor may prescribe a custom-molded helmet or head band. These helmets and bands work best if started between the ages of four and six months, when a child grows the fastest, and will generally be less effective if started after ten months of age. They work by applying gentle but constant pressure on a baby's growing skull in an effort to redirect the growth. These helmets are custom-made and very expensive, costing several thousands of dollars.

Flat Head Syndrome

Parents who carry their babies around most of the time, at least until they can sit, will help their children avoid the problem of flat heads. During this period babies are acquiring the necessary neck muscle strength to hold up their heads.

SIDS Prevention

Wearing your baby is a natural way to prevent sudden infant death syndrome (SIDS). Infants can be worn while they sleep, and none of the acceptable baby-wearing positions, outlined later in this chapter, requires your child to lie on his back while being carried.

Motor Development

Another drawback of infants spending too much time on their backs is that these "container babies"—those who spend long periods in cribs, strollers, car seats, and other restrictive devices—experience delays in motor development.

When lying on their backs, unable to move freely, infants cannot learn and practice motor skills that require antigravity extension (rolling, crawling, sitting, walking). Babies restricted in this way during the first few months of their lives don't grasp, crawl, stand, or walk as early as expected.

The American Physical Therapy Association (APTA)[3] cautions that babies spending too much time on their backs have shown developmental, cognitive, and organizational skills delays, as well as eye-tracking problems and other complications.

Also, investigators in Canada[4] compared motor skills in healthy infants at either four months or six months of age. Two standardized tests were used to evaluate infant motor function, and parents recorded infant positions while their children were awake. All infants were reassessed at 15 months. At four months, infants who had been mostly lying on their backs (supine) had lower motor scores than those who had slept on their tummies (prone), and they were significantly less likely to achieve certain movements of their arms. At six months, differences in motor development between the supine and prone infants increased significantly: 22 percent of the infants who had slept on their backs had overall motor delays and also were less likely to sit and roll. Motor performance also decreased the longer infants spent on their backs in cribs, strollers, or car seats. Even when the babies were evaluated at 15 months, those who had slept on their backs during the first few months showed a delay in overall motor skills such as walking alone and walking up stairs.

Digestion

Babies who are carried enjoy better digestion and spit up less. The upright posture, constant motion, and frequent small feedings keep the baby's stomach contents from passing upward into his esophagus—this is known as gastroesophageal reflux.

Choosing a Carrier

With so many baby carriers available on the market today it can be confusing for parents to make a decision. Here is a look at some of the types out there. In general, each one is suitable for newborns through toddler age.

Slings are pieces of fabric that go over one shoulder. The baby rides in the folds of the fabric close to the body in a variety of positions: front, side, and back. A ring sling is the most speedily adjustable kind of sling to use. A good ring sling enables adjustment to breast height so that the baby can breast-feed easily and discreetly as a mother goes about her daily activities. *When carried in a sling, the baby must be held upright and pressed firmly against the adult's body.*

Wraparounds are made of several yards of cotton-weave material that you wrap around you and your baby, enabling you to wear the baby while distributing his weight along your front, hips, and back. Like slings, wraparounds are often made with beautiful fabrics, weaves, and designs, so they feel more like lovely articles of clothing than pieces of equipment. In a wraparound, your baby is in effect swaddled against your front, which is very calming for the baby. Ideally, a wraparound starts with a belt in front of you in which the baby sits, tummy to tummy. By having the belt in front and the baby positioned in this way, the weight is distributed on your hips and legs, and breast-feeding is easy. Also, as the fabric of a wraparound can be spread across your entire shoulder and back, rather than in a strap width, the 10 percent of the weight that is supported by the upper body is distributed across the entire torso, making it comfortable to wear even for long periods. While you might be daunted at first by the length of the wraparound, they are surprisingly easy to learn.

WEARING YOUR BABY

Carrying your baby is a way to uphold Attachment Parenting International's Ideals of Baby Wearing:[5]

- Baby-wearing helps satisfy the baby's need for closeness, touch, and affection.
- Baby-wearing promotes and strengthens parents' emotional bond with their baby.
- The movement that naturally results from carrying your baby stimulates his neurological development.
- Babies cry less when worn or held.
- Holding helps regulate a baby's temperature and heart rate.
- A baby feels more secure when worn or held.
- Baby-wearing facilitates easy outings and travel.

Soft-structured carriers are easy to use if you'd rather not take the time to learn how to tie a wraparound. In a soft carrier you can hold your baby vertically on either your front, back, or hip. They are suitable for beginners and they don't require any learning; you just clip and go. Men, in particular, tend to prefer the "camping" look afforded by these structured carriers. Newborns are typically carried in the front, often with a cushioned insert that can be placed in the carrier and readjusted as needed, up until the age of four to five months. In this position, it's possible to breast-feed as you go. More heavily structured carriers may have buckles and padded straps as well as a shaped seat. Look for a soft -pack carrier with a wide belt so you can carry tummy to tummy and distribute the baby's weight more evenly onto your hips rather than onto your shoulders and back.

Babies can be carried in front for up to two years, but when breast-feeding becomes less frequent, most mothers find it more pleasurable and practical to carry a heavier child on the back. In soft-structured carriers, the back-carrying position is suitable for babies once they are

Wraparounds, which are made of several yards of cotton-weave material, allow you to evenly distribute your baby's weight across your front, hips, and back.

Men in particular tend to prefer the "camping" look of the soft-structured carriers.

When children get heavier, it's more practical to carry them on your back.

able to sit up on their own and have fully developed neck muscles to support the head properly. Wraparounds are suitable for both front and back carrying even before this, if done correctly. If you're the parent of a child who wants to alternate between being carried and walking, a soft-structured carrier comes in handy because the belt stays buckled around your waist and the shoulder straps can be slid back on within a few seconds. Of the parents experienced in using carriers, most find that the wraparound is incomparable in comfort and versatility, but the structured carriers remain the most practical for those with children who like to frequently go up and down.

A few other things to keep in mind when looking at carriers:

Fabric. A carrier made from organic cotton and non-toxic dyes gives peace of mind when you know that your baby will spend much time in close contact with the fabric.

Proper positioning. Choose a carrier that provides excellent support

When using a carrier on your back, be sure that it supports your child's back.

Charlotte Yonge

for the baby's head, neck, hips, and legs—this is important for the infant's hip, pelvis, and spine growth. An infant carried in a front carrier should always be facing the wearer. If the baby is facing out to the front, the baby will have no leg support, improper spine and hip support, and no head or neck support if he falls asleep.

The carrier's positioning of the baby's legs is critical. Make sure that the ergonomic design of the wrap or front carrier puts the baby in the correct sitting position to encourage proper hip, pelvis, and spine growth. Properly designed carriers will distribute most of the baby's weight between his hips and thighs. When carrying the baby in an upright position, the baby's hips should always be straddled around the wearer's body. The legs should be at least pulled up to a ninety-degree angle. This agrees with the baby's anatomical makeup and supports proper hip development. When carried upright in a soft front pack, babies should never be supported by only a narrow band of fabric at the crotch with their legs dangling. Babies carried in this position do not get enough hip or spine support. The seat of the carrier should be underneath the entire thigh from buttocks to knees to provide support for the hips. Ergonomic carriers put the baby in this position, which supports the legs just as a mother's arms would if the baby were being held in her arms. With the baby's knees bent and the hips spread, it's the most comfortable position for baby and the best for proper hip and spine development. Carriers such as the

Carrying your baby is a way to uphold Attachment Parenting International's Ideals of Baby Wearing.

ERGObaby and wraparound slings appropriately disperse most of the infant's weight between the hips and thighs.

Back Support. The back of the carrier needs to support the baby's back, so that he is not slouching excessively while in the upright position. The carrier needs to be supportive enough so that even when the baby is asleep his body is tightly secured to the wearer's body.

Parent comfort. Ideally the carrier balances the baby's weight along the parents' hips and shoulders, reducing physical stress. Both the wrap and manufactured carriers use wide fabric to cross the shoulders and fit around the waist or on the hips to eliminate back problems for the person carrying the baby.

The Safest Style of Parenting

Another very important reason for keeping your baby close is that this is the best way to keep your baby safe.

Most parents, as consumers with a high level of concern about safety, like to believe that strollers, swings, cribs, and other baby equipment devices have been tested thoroughly. However, unsafe baby products do frequently reach the marketplace, often via reputable manufacturers. The process of pre-market testing is often haphazard and flawed, and many times "approved" products have been found to be dangerous. Notably, while there are mandatory standards for car seats, cribs, rattles, and pacifiers, the safety standards for all other baby equipment are voluntary.

Infant carriers, which typically become rear-facing car seats when placed in a separate base in a motor vehicle, have been responsible for many thousands of injuries when used outside of motor vehicles. Most of the injuries have been related to falls from or within the carrier seat, often from an elevated surface such as a table, counter, or chair.

Similarly, falls from strollers account for the majority of stroller-related injuries, most commonly among babies in the first year. However, there are other common stroller injuries. For instance, in January 2010, the Consumer Product Safety Commission (CPSC) announced a recall of 1.5 million Graco strollers after having received reports of numerous children placing their fingers in the stroller's canopy hinge mechanism while the canopy was being opened or closed, resulting in fingertip lacerations and amputations.

Falls from high chairs, usually from improper restraint, are common as well.

When infant and child equipment are found to be unsafe, consumer product recalls have limited effect. While a recall works well to stop further distribution or sale of a problem product in retail outlets, it falls short in removing problem products from homes and resale shops. The CPSC announces recalls publicly through national television and the Internet, but these announcements often fail to reach families that own and use the product. There is currently no process in place for consumers to be contacted directly by manufacturers about product recalls.

Unsafe baby products frequently reach the marketplace, often via reputable manufacturers. The process of pre-market testing is often haphazard and flawed, and many times "approved" products have been found to be dangerous.

A great majority of the baby gear, although intended to help a mother, actually ends up hindering her by separating her both physically and emotionally from her child and further, by posing various dangers to the child. By limiting your reliance on cribs, strollers, or other expensive, fashionable paraphernalia, you will be doing a world of good for your baby.

Now you know . . .

The safest style of parenting is close parenting, where babies are more often than not held or carried—a tradition that has worked for thousands of years and fortunately is seeing a resurgence today.

FOOTNOTES

1. Hunziker, U.A. and R.G. Barr, "Increased carrying reduces infant crying. A randomized controlled trial," *Pediatrics*, Vol. 77, 641–648.

2. McKinney, C.M., M.L. Cunningham, V.L. Holt, B. Leroux, and J.R. Starr, "Cleft Palate," *Craniofac J*, 2008, Vol. 45, Issue 2, 208–216.

3. "Lack of Time on Tummy shown to Hinder Achievement of Developmental Milestones, Say Physical Therapists," August 6, 2008. American Physical Therapy Association.

4. J. Kemp, "Asymmetric heads and failure to climb stairs," *The Journal of Pediatrics*, Vol. 149, Issue 5, 594–595.

5. © 2001–2004 Attachment Parenting International.

4

Keeping Baby Close: Shared Sleep

PROBABLY NOWHERE do modern Western cultural expectations and the reality of babies' needs conflict more than in the area of sleeping behavior. Babies and their parents sleep together in approximately 90 percent of the world's population. Co-sleeping is simply the "norm" and has been for thousands of years.

In the United States, more and more parents are ignoring warnings of "spoiling" their infants and other dire condemnations of the *family bed*. Instead they are trusting their instincts and are keeping their baby warm and safe at night exactly where nature intended— right next to them. In a poll conducted by *Parenting* magazine,[1] 42 percent of parents responded that they share sleep with their infants at least part of the time.

We cannot "spoil" our babies by always responding to their needs. Babies have an inborn need to be touched and held. They enjoy having physical closeness day and night, and this kind of connection is essential for avoiding stress. The previous chapter discussed how being carried in a carrier or sling during the day meets a baby's needs for warmth, comfort, and security. This dependence does not diminish when the sun goes down.

Many well-meaning family members, friends, and physicians will suggest practices that foster separation between you and your baby in what are largely misguided attempts to force your child to become independent. Practices such as sleep training, scheduled feedings, and "crying it out" only add to your child's distress. Babies whose cries are soothed quickly, for example, tend to cry less, not more.

BED SHARING BENEFITS

Mothers sleep with their children to monitor them and keep them safe, to facilitate breast-feeding, and simply to be near them.

Researchers at the University of Pittsburgh[2] interviewed caregivers who believe that benefits of bed sharing outweigh concerns and warnings, including those of the American Academy of Pediatrics (AAP). Parents identified many benefits of bed sharing:

- Allows both parent and child to sleep better.
- Provides convenience of tending to baby's needs without getting up.
- Gives comfort to parents who enjoy following the tradition.
- Promotes a strong sense of bonding between parents and their children.

In this study, most caregivers expressed their beliefs that bed sharing is protective against SIDS[3] because the parents would immediately know if the baby stopped breathing. Caregivers acknowledged they were not sure how they would know because they would be asleep, but they asserted a strong belief that they would be more likely to identify a lapse in breathing and would wake up if they were physically close to the baby.

Babies who sleep with their parents remain connected to them throughout the night. When they awaken, they can feel the presence of their parent or hear their parent breathing in the dark. Reassured, they go back to sleep.

Co-sleeping is the infant and caregiver sleeping within sensory range of each other (within the same room). *Bed sharing* means that the infant sleeps in the adult bed with at least one parent.[4] A 2005 policy statement by the AAP on sleep environment and the risk of SIDS condemned all bed sharing as unsafe. However, bed sharing is common, and those parents who regularly do so find it to be natural and enjoyable. It is never the bed sharing itself that is unsafe but the way in which it occurs—certain factors are considered to impair safety, such as when a parent's reaction time is somehow weakened, as it would be by drugs or alcohol. A baby co-sleeping with a smoking parent is also a factor associated with more deaths. Soft mattresses, sofa-sleeping, and fluffy bedding must be avoided.

> *Many well-meaning family members, friends, and physicians will suggest practices that foster separation between you and your baby in what are largely misguided attempts to force your child to become independent. Practices such as sleep training, scheduled feedings, and "crying it out" only add to your child's distress.*

Independence

Despite our society's reverence for independence and the belief that children will not become independent unless we force them, babies whose early dependency needs are met are more likely to become trusting, emotionally secure, and *independent when they are ready*.

Human infants need constant attention and contact with other human beings because they are unable to look after themselves. For perhaps millions of years, infants as a matter of course slept next to at least one caregiver, usually the mother, in order to survive. Unlike other mammals, they cannot keep themselves warm, move about, or feed themselves until a relatively long time after birth.

As children get older, they don't need the security of their parents' presence as much and gradually can be weaned from the parents' bed at a time that seems right according to each family's circumstances.

Bed sharing is inherently safe. Many of the publications and articles designed to frighten parents away from keeping babies in bed with them suggest that there is a great risk of rolling over on and suffocating your baby. In May 2002 the Consumer Product Safety Commission (CPSC), in conjunction with the Juvenile Product Manufacturers Association (JPMA), released a recommendation against putting a baby to sleep in an adult bed. This announcement was part of a "national safety campaign." However, it soon became clear that the sponsorship of the campaign by the JPMA—*which stands to profit from increased crib sales*—was nothing but a tremendous marketing campaign to promote cribs and other infant paraphernalia. Pamphlets and posters targeting new and expectant parents were sent to daycare providers and retail outlets of infant products to disseminate the message that infants should sleep in safety-approved cribs only and not in adult beds.

Despite the fact that co-sleeping has been practiced without harm to babies for centuries throughout Asia, Africa, and South America as well as many parts of Europe and North America, mothers are being warned that co-sleeping is causing infant deaths.

The common term for SIDS is "crib death," so named because the great majority of SIDS occurs in infants sleeping alone in cribs, not in bed with their mothers. There is NO evidence that healthy infants habitually sharing a bed with a parent increases the risk of accidental infant suffocation The numbers in the largest study on co-sleeping around the world suggest that with common sense safety factors accounted for, SIDS rates (including suffocations) for co-sleeping infants are actually lower than for crib-sleeping infants.[5]

Each year, hundreds of thousands of cribs are recalled because they can trap or strangle babies. In November 2009—in the largest crib recall in CPSC history—2.2 million Stork Craft drop-side

SAFE BED SHARING

- The mouth and nose must not be obstructed. (Studies showing that sleeping on the back was safer were done in New Zealand where heavy bedding, such as sheepskin, is common.)
- Parents must not smoke nor be impaired by drugs or alcohol (which might diminish your sensitivity to your baby's presence) nor be exhausted from sleep deprivation.
- Parents may not be extremely obese. Parents who are excessively overweight may want to consider using an arrangement in which the baby sleeps in his own space that is attached to the side of the parents' bed.
- Use lightweight covering. Don't use pillows, comforters, quilts, and other soft or plush items on the bed, because they can hinder the breathing of fresh air.
- A firm sleeping surface is needed, which rules out water-beds or soft foam toppers, sofas, or sheepskin covers.
- Make sure the baby cannot become trapped between the mattress and headboard or wall.
- Don't leave your baby alone on an adult bed.

cribs were recalled, including 147,000 cribs with the Fisher-Price logo, after four infants died while trapped in the cribs. Other injuries reported in the wake of this recall included twenty falls from cribs, with injuries ranging from bruises to concussions. In January 2010, 600,000 Dorel cribs (both fixed-side and drop-side) were recalled because of multiple reports of injuries due to entrapment in the slats or between the mattress and the crib. Injuries included scratches, bruises, and death.

In December 2009, the CPSC announced a recall of 24,000 Amby Baby Motion Beds, an infant sleeping device consisting of a steel frame and a fabric hammock, connected by a large spring and metal crossbar. Infant suffocation deaths had occurred when infants became entrapped or wedged against the hammock's fabric or mattress pad. The recalled product could be identified by a label attached to the bed reading, "Amby—Babies Love It, Naturally." In announcing the recall, the CPSC said, "Parents and caregivers are urged to find an alternative, safe sleeping environment for their baby."

As noted earlier, recalls are far more effective for consumers who have not yet purchased the product and as with all other manufacturers of child equipment, crib manufacturers have no mechanism for contacting consumers directly about defective cribs. For instance, a recall of Simplicity-manufactured cribs began in December 2005. Parents and caregivers were advised to dispose of these cribs because of their potential dangers to young children, yet there were reports of baby deaths four years later, in December 2009, due to use of these recalled cribs.

> If one accepts what the studies show—that SIDS is associated with prone sleep positioning, maternal smoking or intoxication, or soft mattress toppers and heavy or fluffy bedding that could potentially suffocate the baby—then avoidance of these situations while bed sharing can help create a particularly safe sleeping environment.

The CPSC, a consumer *product* safety commission, has no mandate to tell parents where and how their babies should sleep, particularly when non-bed sharing arrangements—as shown by these recalls—can be dangerous. A public health initiative to educate parents about safe co-sleeping for parents who choose to do so would be a far greater contribution to child welfare than scaring parents into buying cribs or "hammocks" and other isolating devices that have the potential to be unsafe.

Research shows that it is not bed sharing itself but rather other factors in and around the sleeping space that create danger. If one accepts what the studies show—that SIDS is associated with prone sleep positioning, maternal smoking or intoxication, or soft mattress toppers and heavy or fluffy bedding that could potentially suffocate the baby—then avoidance of these situations while bed sharing can help create a *particularly safe* sleeping environment.

Responsible parents who practice authentic bed sharing do not sleep with a baby if they smoke, drink, or take drugs. Any other caution against bed sharing directly contradicts most cultures and interferes with bonding between mother and child. And there is no need to spend your money on gadgets that mimic a mother's heartbeat or breathing motions. The real thing is free.

Breast-feeding

Co-sleeping encourages breast-feeding by making nighttime breast-feeding more convenient, and the combination helps babies fall asleep more easily, especially during their first few months when they wake up in the middle of the night.

The AAP counsels that breast-feeding is an important factor in SIDS prevention and acknowledges that bed sharing facilitates breast-feeding and mother-baby bonding.[6]

The AAP admonition that a breast-feeding infant *never* sleep in the mother's bed[7] appears to be an ironic contradiction that in practice is likely to have an adverse effect on breast-feeding and serve to increase the rate of SIDS. When a baby is nursing frequently during the night, it is much easier for mothers to nurse for a while and then fall back to sleep with their babies. Mothers who have to get out of bed to nurse can be expected to suffer significantly more fatigue getting fully awake to fetch the baby and then putting the baby back to bed after each feed. Breast-feeding in these cases is more likely to be diminished or given up altogether.

Plagiocephaly

Plagiocephaly or flat-head syndrome was discussed previously in Chapter 3: when babies sleep on their backs, as recommended by the AAP, they are likely to develop flat heads, as the bones of the

DEVELOPMENTAL DELAYS LINKED TO BABIES SLEEPING ON THEIR BACKS

An important study reported in *Pediatrics* in February 2010 confirmed that babies who have misshapen heads from lying on their backs are twice as likely to experience significant delayed physical and mental development compared to babies who did not have deformed skulls.[8]

The study, which reviewed 427 babies, aged four months to 1 year, showed that those with flat-head syndrome had lower scores on tests of cognitive and motor skills development. The tests included simple tasks of problem-solving and memory (such as finding a hidden toy) ability to imitate, vocalize, observe, and respond to environment; and motor skills such as crawling or rolling from side to side, and being able to lift up from a tummy position.

While it was pointed out in Chapter 3 that large numbers of infants are now wearing corrective helmets as well as undergoing unnecessary tests and even surgery, this study points out that simply correcting the head shape is only addressing the cosmetic issue, and leaves out the larger concern of the baby's development.

The study findings suggest that positional plagiocephaly is more than just a cosmetic concern.

This research, done at Seattle Children's Hospital, was funded by the National Institute of Child Health and Human Development and the National Center for Research Resources.

While it was pointed out in Chapter 3 that large numbers of infants are now wearing corrective helmets as well as undergoing unnecessary tests and even surgery, this study points out that simply correcting the head shape is only addressing the cosmetic issue, and leaves out the larger concern of the baby's development.

skull remain relatively soft and malleable for months after birth. In contrast, a sleeping infant who nurses during the night changes position several times as a mother switches her baby from one side to the other. This natural changing of back- and side-lying positions helps develop a properly-formed skull.

Now you know . . .

Safe bed sharing, when done properly, is a practice that does not harm babies and, when combined with breast-feeding, can yield numerous benefits for you and your child.

FOOTNOTES

1. Onderko, Patty, "Crib-Sleeping vs. Co-Sleeping: Where does your baby spend the night?" *Babytalk*, www.parenting.com/article/Baby/Care/Crib-Sleeping-Vs-Co-Sleeping.
2. Chianese, J., M.D., M.S., D. Ploof, Ed.D., C. Trovato, Ph.D., J.C. Chang, M.D, M.PH.,"Inner-City Caregivers' Perspectives on Bed Sharing With Their Infants," *Academic Pediatrics*,2009, Vol. 9, Issue 1, 26–32.
3. SIDS is the abbreviation for sudden infant death syndrome that in common usage is interchanged with infant suffocation, although they are not in actuality the same thing.
4. According to Dr. James McKenna, an anthropologist and director of the University of Notre Dame Mother-Baby Behavioral Sleep Lab.
5. Nelson, E.A., "International Child Care Practices Study: infant sleeping environment," *Early Hum Dev.*, April 2001, Vol. 62, Issue 1, 43–55.
6. Hauck, F. R., et al., "Bed sharing promotes breast-feeding and AAP Task Force on Infant Positioning and SIDS," *Pediatrics*, 1998, Vol. 102, Issue 3, Part 1: 662–4. 4.
7. "There is no evidence that co-sleeping can be done safely," John Kattwinkel, M.D., chairperson of the AAP's Task Force on SIDS.
8. Speltz, M., et al., "Case-control study of neurodevelopment in deformational plagiocephaly," *Pediatrics*, 2010; DOI: 10.1542/peds.2009-0052.

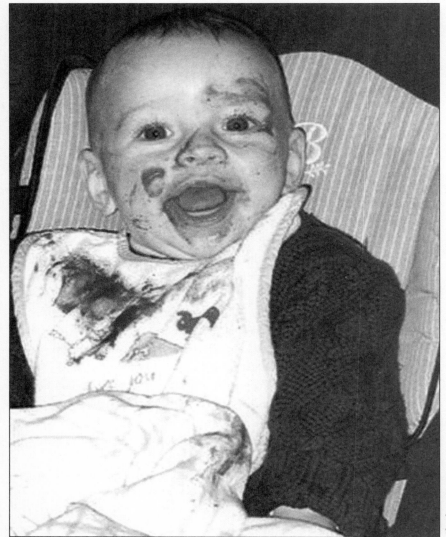

5

Nutrition

"Let medicine be thy food, and let food be thy medicine."
—HIPPOCRATES

*"Children are more harmed by poor diet than by exposure to
alcohol, drugs, and tobacco combined."*
—DAVID KATZ, M.D.,
Yale University Medical Center[1]

MULTIBILLION DOLLAR ADVERTISING for unhealthy processed
foods and other junk food, targeted at parents and their children, has
successfully changed what we consider to be "normal" in terms of
what we eat and what we feed our children. The resulting widespread
disease—an overall lack of health and well-being—is creating children who are not achieving their physical and mental potential and
who, in some cases, end up seeking medical treatment for maladies
that good nutrition would have prevented. Good, wholesome food is
the most important factor in your child's health and well being.

The Beginning

As noted earlier, exclusive breast-feeding for the first six months,
with continued breast-feeding for at least one or two years, is a strong

iStock

Continued breast-feeding is the basis for optimal infant and child health.

foundation for optimal infant and child health. Human milk is simply remarkable, and no artificial formula can touch its nutritional value.

Meeting in Florence, Italy in July 1990, government policy-makers from more than thirty countries, including the United States, adopted the Innocenti Declaration on the Protection, Promotion, and Support of Breast-feeding. This declaration states that of all contributors to an infant's life, breast-feeding is the most valuable. It recognizes that breast-feeding is a unique process that:

1. provides ideal nutrition for infants
2. contributes to healthy infant growth and development
3. reduces the instance and severity of infectious diseases, thereby lowering infant mortality and morbidity (incidence of disease)
4. contributes to women's health by reducing the risk of breast and ovarian cancer, and by increasing the time between pregnancies.
5. provides social and economic benefits to the family and the nation.

6. provides most women with a sense of satisfaction when successfully carried out.

In addition, the benefits of breast-feeding increase:

- when the baby is fed breast milk *only* (exclusive breast-feeding) during the first six months.
- the longer it is continued even after complementary foods are added at four to six months.

Starting Solids

You'll find that there are many different opinions regarding the best time to start your baby on solid foods. As a result of extensive research, many health professionals and such health agencies as World Health Organization (WHO) and the American Academy of Pediatrics (AAP) now recognize that breast milk is the most important food for young babies and provides all the calories and essential nutrients for healthy growth until age six months. As such, parents are encouraged to wait at least until then before starting solids. Even at the age of six months, if your baby isn't interested in eating solids, do not force the issue. Go back to nursing exclusively for a few weeks before trying again. It is more important that you both enjoy mealtimes than for your baby to start solids by a specific date.

> *Try to get fresh, organic fruits and vegetables. There is no need to purchase expensively packaged commercial baby food.*

Once your baby starts eating solid foods, serve foods in as close to their natural state as possible. Try to get fresh, organic fruits and vegetables. There is no need to purchase expensively packaged commercial baby food.

When the baby is starting to eat solid food at about six months, there is no medical evidence that introducing foods in any particular order has any advantage for your baby. You can start with mashed avocado or mashed banana. Steamed vegetables such as broccoli, carrots, squash, or sweet potatoes take just a few minutes to prepare and can be mashed to the correct consistency with a fork.

It was previously thought that "high allergen" foods such as eggs, wheat, and foods containing peanut protein should be avoided until the baby was at least a year old. However, there's no current convincing evidence that delaying the introduction of these foods beyond the age of six months affects whether or not your child gets allergies. For instance, a study reported in the January 2010 issue of *Pediatrics* found that late introduction of solid foods was associated with *increased* risk of later allergy—both to foods and to inhaled substances.[2]

Also, babies younger than six months should not be given juice. It is often sugar-laden water with little nutritional value and can interfere with breast-feeding.

Between the First and Second Birthday

A child's growth slows considerably after the first year. After tripling their birth weight by the first birthday, babies gain only a few pounds during the second year. Because growth rate slows, appetite slows as well. Surprised parents often express concern to the pediatrician about how little the baby eats at this stage. However, as long as your child's energy level is normal and he's growing normally, there's no reason to be alarmed, and trying to force extra calories is counterproductive. Even though toddlers are very active, they simply require fewer calories per pound than infants.

While it may seem like your toddler doesn't eat enough, is never hungry, or won't eat unless spoon-fed, don't worry. Your child's appetite is just naturally slowing down.

While it may seem like your toddler doesn't eat enough, is never hungry, or won't eat unless spoon-fed, don't worry. Your child's appetite is just naturally slowing down.

GROWTH CHARTS

Children grow at different rates. Some children can develop very quickly, others more slowly. This is usually not a reflection of your child's health. In the first few months, breast-fed babies often can be heavier than artificially fed infants. Later in the first year, breast-fed children are often thinner than those who are bottle fed. After six months, the build of a child is generally dependent on characteristics inherited from the parents rather than how much or little the child is eating.

By the time parents bring their babies in for his first well-child checkup, they've probably been conditioned to wonder—and worry—about where their child fits on the "growth chart" and how their babies compare to other babies of the same age. While it's natural to want to make sure that your baby's height and weight are normal, it's also important to understand the value—and the shortcomings—of the growth chart.

Two different representative growth charts are available for use in pediatricians' offices and your child's doctor is probably using the "old" kind.[2] Most U.S. pediatricians currently use the CDC/Center for Health Statistics growth charts, based on a set of babies weighed and measured in the United States. However, at the time data for these charts were collected, most children in the United States were *not exclusively breast-fed*. The growth curves were developed by the CDC in 2000 and describe how babies and children grew across a wide range of social, ethnic, and economic conditions, using data from infants in the 1970s and 1980s. During this period, only one-third of American infants were breast-fed up to age three months, while the other two-thirds were predominantly formula-fed. None of the babies were exclusively breast-fed for six months. Currently the AAP, the American Academy of Family Physicians, and the U.S. Surgeon General all recommend *exclusive breast-feeding until six months* of age. Thus, at the time the CDC data was collected, very few mothers were feeding their babies in the optimal manner currently recommended.

On April 27, 2006, the World Health Organization (WHO) charts became available in the United States. These WHO standard curves describe how infants should grow under the ideal conditions of being breast-fed. The cross-sectional data from the WHO 2006 curves includes 6,669 young children who were breast-fed for at least three months.

If all pediatricians were to switch to the WHO growth chart, the normal weight-gain pattern of breast-fed babies would be better represented. Because healthy breast-fed infants tend to grow more rapidly than formula-fed infants in the first two to three months, and less rapidly from three to twelve months, a breast-fed baby who is measured according to the CDC chart is more likely to be labeled "underweight." The pediatrician might even suggest supplements, even though the baby appears to be perfectly healthy. If growth charts were based on breast-fed infants, many bottle fed infants would be diagnosed as overweight.

> *A breast-fed baby who is measured according to the CDC chart is more likely to be labeled "underweight."... If growth charts were based on breast-fed infants, many bottle fed infants would be diagnosed as overweight.*

The new growth chart standards are based on the breast-fed child as the norm for growth and development. For the first time, this aligns the tools used to assess growth with the national and international infant feeding guidelines that recommend breast-feeding as the optimal source of nutrition during infancy.

It is also important to understand that the growth chart used by your pediatrician may not be appropriate for your own baby in other ways, because it does not take into account the child's individual feeding patterns or the parents' height and ethnicity.

Though it's often not the case, a pediatrician should be looking to see that a baby stays relatively consistent in his *growth pattern*, not that he be at a specific percentile for weight or height on the chart during any given visit.

Observing your baby is much more important than looking at numbers on a piece of paper. No matter how your baby measures up, it is most important that your baby is gaining weight and growing over time, is meeting developmental milestones, and is happy, alert, and active.

"My Child Doesn't Eat"

Parents of toddlers or preschoolers frequently ask the pediatrician how to handle a child who "won't eat." However, the child in question is invariably well-nourished, happy, and developing normally. This is not a time for the pediatrician to suggest any kind of manufactured calorie-boosting nutritional supplement drinks. These are loaded with additives and preservatives and do not teach proper nutrition. (The first three ingredients of Pediasure are water, sugar, and maltodextrin, a common food additive.)

> *Based on the number of calories, milk is a food, not a drink, and children simply get too full to eat anything else.*

Children do not starve. As long as they have access to food, they have a natural ability to satisfy their energy needs for activity and growth. The difference is that *children eat when they are hungry*, a more natural way than eating according to the clock or social cues. It's normal for toddlers and preschoolers to want to take little bits of food throughout the day rather than eating most of their food at designated mealtimes.

One common and potentially troubling reason that some toddlers "don't eat" is that they are drinking too much cow's milk. Based on the number of calories, milk is a food, not a drink, and children simply get too full to eat anything else. If parents say "but my child loves milk," that is, in fact, the problem. Some toddlers who love milk would drink it all day, but too much is not good for them.

You'll see in the next chapter that cow's milk is not a healthy food for children. Often mothers are so worried that their toddler is not eating that they are happy to give him more milk—but that only exacerbates the problem. If you can't cut out cow's milk altogether, try to limit your child to no more than two cups daily. Another mistake is giving a child unhealthy, empty-calorie food just to ensure he's eating *something*.

A small child weighs only a fraction of what an adult weighs, and requires proportionately less food. Sometimes parents don't realize how little food a child really needs. It can be overwhelming for a child to be presented with what seems like a mountain of food on his plate.

Never force your child to eat. Forcing children to eat teaches them to ignore their body's natural signals that tell them when they're hungry or full. It also takes all the fun out of eating. Your best bet is to provide healthy food for snacks and meals and allow your child to eat what he wants, when he wants it. As long as your child consumes a reasonable quantity and variety of foods over the course of a week, he'll be fine. Eating small, more frequent meals is perfectly normal for children. If your child is not eating any food at all at mealtimes, make sure that you are allowing enough time between snacks and meals for him to become sufficiently hungry.

> *Never force your child to eat. Forcing children to eat teaches them to ignore their body's natural signals that tell them when they're hungry or full. It also takes all the fun out of eating.*

Juice

If your child doesn't eat, milk is not the only culprit. Juice could also be the reason. Some kids would drink juice all day long if you let them, but too much juice can take the place of more nutritious foods as well as promote tooth decay. When it comes to reasons why you'd want to give your child juice, nutrition isn't one of them.

Juice should not be considered a substitute for your child's need for fresh fruit. Juice does contain some vitamins and minerals, but it has far less than whole fruit. Whole fruit also contains fiber while juice does not.

To start cutting your child back on juice, you can quietly begin diluting his servings with water. Given the sweetness of many juice products he likely won't ever notice the difference.

The Standard American Diet (SAD)

The Standard American Diet consists of processed foods, red meat, fried foods, soft drinks, refined carbohydrates, and food additives. It's perhaps all too fitting that the acronym for this "diet" is "S.A.D."

Many Americans consume too many calories as well as too much fat, especially saturated fat, trans fat, and cholesterol. Getting back to our roots of food fresh from the earth is not easy when living in a fast-food society that has us eating foods that are overcooked, over-processed, hormone injected, and loaded with antibiotics. The World Health Organization (WHO) recognizes the standard American diet as contributing to obesity, diabetes, cancer, and heart disease.[4]

Moreover, children have specific and complex nutritional needs that are not met with this regimen. Many of the over-manufactured, packaged foods ingested by the typical American child are vitamin

> Sugary donuts and cereal can affect a child's ability to pay attention and cause irritability. Artificial colors, flavors, and preservatives may contribute to difficulty with thinking, coordination, and memory.

and mineral deficient and full of pesticides. Vitamin content is further compromised by freezing, frying, and overcooking the food. And the effects of some of the diet's harmful ingredients are quite specific: sugary donuts and cereal can affect a child's ability to pay attention and cause irritability. Artificial colors, flavors, and preservatives may well also contribute to difficulty with thinking, coordination, and memory.

Think again about what comprises the Standard American Diet—processed food, red meat, fried food, soft drinks, refined carbs, and food additives. It is sobering to think that you can probably hit all aspects of that diet—taking in staggering amounts of fat, calories, and salt—during one hastily considered fast-food meal.

Nutritious Foods vs. Enriched Foods

Serve and cook real foods: the closer the food is to its natural state (a "whole food"), the better it is for your child. Eliminate manufactured foods, chemicals, and known allergens from your diet.

Nutritious foods have not been processed or refined. They are free of additives, such as colorings and preservatives, and they have not

When kids experiment in the kitchen, encourage them to use real foods, not enriched products.

Charlotte Yonge

been modified. Often, as a result of processing, food loses important vitamins and minerals, and, consequently, many of its health benefits.

Examples of whole foods are fruits, vegetables, nuts, seeds, eggs, chicken, and fish. The difference between a whole food and a processed food is the difference between a baked potato and a bag of potato chips.

Be wary of foods that have been "enriched." Usually that means that something bad has happened to the food during processing, depleting it of nutrients; then, in a clever marketing ploy, something of little value has been added to make up for the depleted nutrients. All too often, these "enrichments" are bad for a person's health.

> The difference between a whole food and a processed food is the difference between a baked potato and a bag of potato chips.

Hydrogenated Oils and Trans Fats

When hydrogen is added to oil to harden it, the result is an artificial trans fat. In 1911, Crisco was the first commercial product to employ *partial hydrogenation* of plant oils. Many more manufacturers started including trans fat–laden hydrogenated oil in their processed foods in the 1980s, producing both hydrogenated and partially hydrogenated oils to improve the texture and shelf life of their products. However, these artificial fats—often found lurking in abundance in cookies, cakes, doughnuts, crackers, icing, potato chips, stick margarine, and microwave popcorn—clog arteries and cause obesity. Quite simply, avoid all foods that list hydrogenated or partially hydrogenated fats or shortenings on their labels. Fortunately, in 2006, the U.S. Food and Drug Administration began requiring food manufacturers to disclose their products' trans fats, which are listed under the fat category of the product's nutrition facts panel.

Many foods are now formulated to be trans-fat free, and many packages of snack foods, cookies, and crackers in the grocery aisles declare "zero grams trans fat." However, bear in mind that *zero* does not mean "none." Federal regulations permit manufacturers to say there are zero grams of trans fat as long as there's less than half a gram *per serving*. Yet many manufacturers get around this by designating as one serving an amount that is quite clearly unrealistic as a single serving. Most people, children included, eat far more than this "serving" from any given package of food during a single sitting.

> Bear in mind that zero does not mean "none." Federal regulations permit manufacturers to say there are zero grams of trans fat as long as there's less than half a gram per serving. Yet many manufacturers get around this by designating as one serving an amount that is quite clearly unrealistic as a single serving.

The point is, these small amounts of "zero" trans fat can add up. Remember again that you're scanning the nutrition panel for some mention of hydrogenated oil, as the words "trans fat" may not be present on the packaging, except if there's a claim of "no trans fats." In which case, check the ingredient panel anyway. The American Heart Association recommends that people limit trans fats to less than two grams per day. Other health researchers suggest that it should be less than one gram. The best amount would be a true zero.

Supplements

If as a parent you fear your child's diet is somehow lacking in vitamins and minerals you might be tempted to give him vitamin and mineral supplements to compensate.

Although supplements are not in themselves harmful, parents sometimes rely on them to the point of getting lax about their child's eating habits, thinking that a daily gummy will make up for any diet deficiencies. Keep in mind that real, whole food has been minimally processed and contains a virtual natural pharmacy of nutrients, phytochemicals, enzymes, vitamins, minerals, antioxidants, anti-inflammatories, and healthful fats that can help your child thrive.

A healthy, well-balanced diet with some variety is far more important than most vitamin and mineral supplements; plus, these supplements are often costly. A bottle of one hundred multivitamin-mineral tablets for children can cost about $10, and nearly $2 *billion* is spent on them annually.

> *Whole food has been minimally processed and contains a virtual natural pharmacy of nutrients, phytochemicals, enzymes, vitamins, minerals, antioxidants, anti-inflammatories, and healthful fats that can help your child thrive.*

Essential Nutrients

Vitamin A plays a vital role in the growth and repair of human body tissue. It is particularly important in maintaining good eyesight and healthy skin, as well as aiding in proper bone and teeth formation. Foods rich in vitamin A include eggs, fish, sweet potatoes, carrots, cantaloupe, broccoli, mangoes, apricots, and dark greens such as kale, spinach, and romaine lettuce.

Vitamin B12 is necessary for cell division and blood formation. The adult recommended intake for vitamin B12 is very low. The vitamin comes primarily from animal-derived foods. Dairy products or eggs will provide an adequate amount in your diet. Non-animal sources of vitamin B12 include cereals, breads, nutritional yeast, and some fortified soy products. Check the labels for the words cyanocobalamin or B12. Tempeh and sea vegetables may contain vitamin B12, but their content varies and may be unreliable. Fortified soy milk and fortified breakfast cereals also have this important vitamin. To be on the safe side, if your family consumes no dairy products, eggs, or fortified foods, you can take a non-animal derived B12 supplement.

DO NOT USE TEFLON (NONSTICK) COOKWARE

Teflon-coated pans emit toxic gases when heated. Perfluorinated chemicals—better known as PFC's—are used to make these nonstick coatings, and these chemicals can accumulate in the body. The EPA lists PFOA (one type of PFCs used in Teflon) as a "likely human carcinogen." Teflon is perhaps the best-known non-stick term but nonstick coatings are also advertised under such names as Fluoron, Supra, Excalibur, Greblon, Xylon, Duracote, Resistal, and Autograph, and they are incorporated into various brands of cookware in the marketplace.

Pet birds have died in kitchens where nonstick cookware was being used. The Environmental Working Group (EWG) has found that pans with nonstick coating can turn toxic in two to five minutes when heated on a typical household stove, producing toxins that even DuPont acknowledges kill hundreds of birds each year. Once the bird inhales the toxic fumes, death is almost instantaneous.

DuPont and other companies have agreed, in response to government pressure, to eliminate use of PFOA by 2015. You might want to eliminate it from your home sooner.

Vitamin C (ascorbic acid) assists the body in the production of collagen, a basic component of connective tissues. Collagen is an important structural element in blood vessel walls, gums, and bones. Vitamin C also acts as an antioxidant, scavenging your child's body for potentially harmful molecules called free radicals. This antioxidant capacity also may help boost your child's immune system. Foods high in vitamin C include oranges and other citrus fruits, berries, kiwi, broccoli, dark greens, melons, and tomatoes.

Vitamin D is named "the sunshine vitamin." Very few foods in nature contain significant amounts of vitamin D because this fat-soluble substance is manufactured in the skin upon exposure to ultraviolet

B (UVB) rays. In fact, these properties are why it's really a hormone and not a vitamin meant to be obtained through food. Vitamin D has long been considered an important nutrient because it helps the body absorb calcium, but more and more research is linking insufficient vitamin D levels to diabetes, cardiovascular disease, autoimmune disease, inflammatory illnesses, and even some cancers.[5] Far from only being necessary for bone formation, sufficient vitamin D is imperative for proper immune function, neuromuscular function, and brain development.

A normal and easy way for you and your child's skin to soak up adequate levels of vitamin D is to spend a little time in the sun. How long? The factors that affect ultraviolet radiation exposure (season, geographic latitude, time of day, cloud cover, smog, and skin melanin content, i.e., skin color) make it difficult to provide exact guidelines that work for everyone, but according to the National Institutes of Health (NIH), ten to fifteen minutes of direct sunlight at least twice a week to the face, arms, hands, or back is sufficient to maintain optimum serum vitamin D levels.[6] Oily fish such as salmon, tuna, and mackerel contain ample amounts of vitamin D, while beef liver and egg yolks have small amounts.

> *10 to 15 minutes of direct sunlight at least twice a week to the face, arms, hands, or back is generally sufficient to maintain optimum serum vitamin D levels.*

Calcium is important for strong, healthy bones. There are many calcium-rich, non-dairy foods such as broccoli and dark green leafy vegetables, both of which are also great sources of vitamin K, another key nutrient for bone health. Sardines, salmon, kiwi, rhubarb, nuts, beans, chickpeas, lentils, split peas, yams, dried figs, blackstrap molasses, sesame seeds, and tofu are just a few of the many other nutrient-dense foods that can help meet your body's calcium needs.

Iron enables optimal oxygen transport in red blood cells. Good iron sources include legumes (chickpeas, soybeans, lentils, and baked beans), tofu, spinach, pumpkin seeds, broccoli, blackstrap molasses,

PHYTOCHEMICALS: THE UNSUNG ANTIOXIDANTS

Phytochemicals are an important aspect of the human diet. They are non-caloric plant chemicals that have protective or disease-preventive properties. "Phyto" is a Greek word for plant life, and the phytochemicals are a very broad range of substances found in plants that we eat. Most foods, except those that are heavily refined, such as sugar, contain one form of phytochemical or another. The primary sources of these substances are fruits, vegetables, and most beans.

But here's the twist. Phyochemicals themselves don't have any nutritional value and are not required by the human body for sustaining life. What they do provide is antioxidant activity, which protects our body's cells against oxidative damage and reduces the risk of developing certain types of cancer. Some well-known phytochemicals are:

- allyl sulfides (onions, leeks, garlic)
- carotenoids (fruits, carrots)
- flavonoids (fruits, vegetables, onions, tea)
- polyphenols (tea, grapes)
- lycopene (tomatoes, pink grapefruit, guava, watermelon)

bulgur, prune juice, and dried fruit (raisins and figs). Eating these foods along with foods high in vitamin C (citrus fruits and juices, tomatoes, oranges, strawberries, and broccoli) increases the amount of iron your body can absorb. Believe it or not, cooking food in iron cookware also adds to your iron intake.

Zinc is an important trace mineral, second only to iron in its concentration in the body. It is necessary for proper functioning of the body's immune system, and it plays a role in protein synthesis, cell division, and wound healing. Zinc is also needed for the senses of smell and taste. A daily intake of zinc is required to maintain a steady state because the body has no specialized zinc storage system. Make sure that dried beans, nuts, wheat germ, and soy products like tofu and tempeh are part of your family's diet in order to meet the daily requirement for this important mineral.

Lecithin, a special type of fat-soluble nutrient called a phospholipid, is a very powerful brain food. Lecithin contains the B vitamin choline, which helps promote your child's brain development and also boosts memory and concentration. Lecithin is found naturally in a number of foods, including egg yolk, fish, grains, legumes, peanuts, soybeans, wheat germ, and yeast.

Protein helps children grow, but they do not need to get it from high-protein, animal-based foods. Many people are unaware that a varied menu of grains, beans, vegetables, and fruits supplies plenty of protein—this means children can get protein while on a vegetarian diet. In fact it would be very difficult to design a vegetarian diet that is short on protein. Excess dietary protein may lead to health problems. It is now thought that one of the benefits of a vegetarian diet is that it contains adequate but not excessive protein. Some people believe that vegetarians must combine incomplete plant proteins in one meal—like red beans and rice—to make the type of complete proteins found in meat. We now know that it's not that complicated. It's not necessary to plan combinations of foods to obtain enough protein or amino acids (components of protein). A mixture of plant proteins eaten throughout the day will provide enough essential amino acids. Good protein sources are beans, tofu, nuts, seeds, tempeh (fermented soy), and peas.

> *It's not necessary to plan combinations of foods to obtain enough protein or amino acids (components of protein). A mixture of plant proteins eaten throughout the day will provide enough essential amino acids.*

Essential fatty acids (EFAs) are required by infants and toddlers for proper development—cells, hormones, and neurotransmitters

SOURCES OF OMEGA-3 FOR VEGETARIANS

Getting enough of the ALA omega-3 fat can be a challenge for vegetarians, especially vegans. Though they don't eat fish, vegetarians can, of course, eat algae directly. Algae such as chlorella and spirulina provide valuable sources of these converted fats as well as a whole host of other nutrients. Another good source of ALA in the vegetarian diet—the simplest source—is flaxseed oil, taken either on its own or mixed into dressings and other foods. Most of the small amount of fat in leafy green vegetables such as broccoli and cabbage is ALA, which can also be found in hemp and pumpkin seeds and walnuts.

---

are built from fat and protein. Fully 60 percent of a child's brain and nervous system is made of fat.

Alpha-linolenic acid (ALA) is an omega-3 fat that is a precursor of the longer chain omega-3 fats eicosapentaenoic acid (EPA) and docosahexaenoic acid (DHA). In other words, the human body converts the ALA omega-3 fat into the even more beneficial EPA and DHA fats. Among its many roles, EPA is needed for brain function, concentration, and vision, and is also converted into a powerful anti-inflammatory agent. DHA is needed for brain structure and thus is especially important for the baby's brain and nervous system development. These two fatty acids are the ones available in significant amounts in oily fish and fish oil supplements (fish convert the essential fats from algae into these fats and then accumulate them up the food chain).

The body can synthesize some of the fats it needs from foods. However, EFAs must come from your diet; they cannot be synthesized in the body. EFAs such as omega-3 fatty acids are the beneficial or "healthy fats" that kids need in abundance for learning, coordination, fine motor skills, immune strength, skin health, mood regulation, and overall emotional health and mental development.

CONTAMINATED FISH:
AN UNHEALTHY BYPRODUCT
OF HUMAN POLLUTION

In general, fish is considered an exceptionally good food for infants and children. It contains highly usable protein, the omega-3 fatty acids DHA and EPA, and other nutrients. However, mercury pollution from coal-fired power plants has resulted in widespread contamination of fish with toxic mercury that far outweighs its nutritional benefits. Besides mercury, unacceptable levels of dioxins and PCPs have often been found in fish destined for the food chain.

Mercury from power plants moves through the air, is deposited in water, and finds its way into fish. Some fish and shellfish tend to contain higher levels, either because they live in more contaminated waters or because they are larger carnivores consuming many contaminated smaller fish. Large predator fish that are higher up the food chain—like swordfish, cod, tuna, sea bass, marlin, halibut, and sharks—show some of the worst contamination.

Mercury exposure has been linked to a wide variety of ills, including acute and chronic effects on the cardiovascular and central nervous systems. Also, the Environmental Protection Agency (EPA) and the International Agency for Research on Cancer (IARC) have designated mercury as a possible human carcinogen.

Children under 6, as well as women who are pregnant or planning to become pregnant, are the most vulnerable to mercury's harmful effects.

EFAs are readily available in breast milk, so infant formula manufacturers as well as baby food companies are now adding EFAs to their products in their efforts to imitate mother's milk. However, at least one study shows that supplementing infant formula with fatty acids had no impact on the developmental scores of 18-month-olds, pointing to the fact that EFA supplementation does not effectively emulate breast milk.[7]

> *Mercury pollution from coal-fired power plants has resulted in widespread contamination of fish with toxic mercury that far outweighs its nutritional benefits.*

While EFAs are available from small cold-water fatty fish (especially sardines, salmon, and herring), be wary of mercury contamination when consuming fish, especially big carnivorous fish like swordfish and shark.

But fish consumption is not the only way to ensure an adequate intake of essential fatty acids. Many healthful foods from plant sources offer the full range of essential nutrients found in fish without the potential toxins and other health risks from certain fish. The most nutritious sources of EFAs in plant-based foods are green leafy vegetables, avocado, beans, nuts (such as walnuts and almonds), seeds (such as pumpkin, sunflower, hemp, and flax), fruits, and whole grains. EFAs are also found in such oils derived from flax, canola, soybean, walnut, and wheat germ.

Vegetarian Diets

Albert Einstein said, "Nothing will benefit human health and increase chances of survival for life on earth as much as the evolution to a vegetarian diet."

A vegetarian diet is defined as one that does not include meat (including fowl) or seafood, or products containing those foods. In the past, choosing this diet was considered unusual in the United States, but times and attitudes have changed. Vegetarian diets are becoming increasingly mainstream, and more families, children included, are starting to make the switch.

Why bother raising your child with a vegetarian lifestyle? Because it can drastically decrease the chance of your child getting heart disease, diabetes, and cancer, and will make your child less prone to obesity, assuming a healthy exercise regimen is also followed. Studies show that vegetarian children, contrary to common belief, grow as tall as omnivorous (both plant and animal eating) children, and sometimes even taller. Other studies show that vegetarian

Fotolia

children have higher IQs, with averages as high as 116. Furthermore, vegetarian diets have been found to decrease the prevalence of allergies and gastrointestinal problems. By avoiding meat, your child will not only realize the potential of a healthier lifestyle but will also avoid the pesticides and toxins that can accumulate in animals at the top of the food chain.

The American Dietetic Association (ADA) has officially endorsed vegetarianism. In July 2009, the ADA released an updated position paper that states that vegetarian diets, if well-planned, are healthful and nutritious for all age groups and can help prevent as well as treat chronic diseases:

> It is the position of the American Dietetic Association that appropriately planned vegetarian diets, including total vegetarian or vegan diets, are healthful, nutritionally adequate, and may provide health

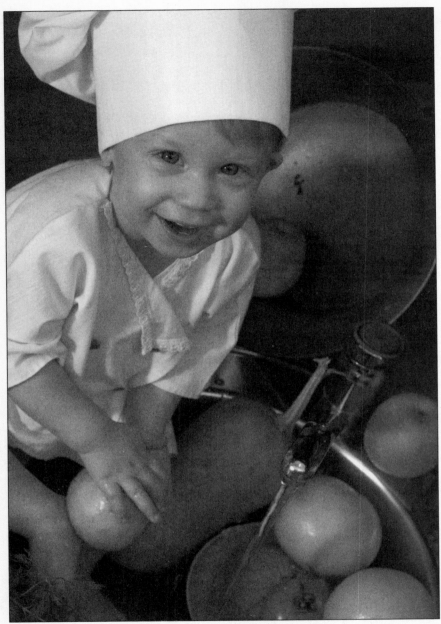

iStock

In order for your child's vegetarian diet to be a success, he needs to get a range of healthful foods, including fruits, vegetables, plenty of leafy greens, nuts, seeds, and legumes.

benefits in the prevention and treatment of certain diseases. Well-planned vegetarian diets are appropriate for individuals during all stages of life, including pregnancy, lactation, infancy, childhood, and adolescence, and for athletes.[8]

Likewise, doctors and dietitians at the nonprofit organization Physicians Committee for Responsible Medicine (PCRM) state that well-planned vegetarian diets are healthy choices for pregnant women and their children, saying, "Vegetarian diets offer a number of nutritional benefits, including lower levels of saturated fat and cholesterol and higher levels of fiber, folate, and cancer-fighting antioxidants and phytochemicals."[9]

The American Dietetic Association broadly defines three types of vegetarian diets:

- Lacto-ovo vegetarian diet: okay to eat eggs and dairy.
- Lacto-vegetarian diet: okay to have dairy but not eggs.
- Vegan or total vegetarian diet: not okay to eat eggs or dairy.

The key to a healthy vegetarian diet, as with any other diet, is to eat a wide variety of healthful foods, including fruits, vegetables, plenty of leafy greens, nuts, seeds, and legumes.

The most important element of a vegetarian baby's diet is breast milk. For the first six months, breast milk supplies all that a child needs

> *Vegetarian mothers have been found to have lower pesticide residues in their milk.*

nutritionally. Breast milk should be offered for the first two years, especially to vegan children. Vegetarian mothers have been found to have lower pesticide residues in their milk.

Solids can be introduced to vegetarian infants at the same stage and pace as for omnivore infants. After the age of six months, vegetarian babies can be offered fruits (fresh or dried) and vegetables, and protein sources like mashed tofu, avocado (sliced or mashed), pureed beans and legumes, and nut and seed butters.

Concerns about Soy

Soy and soy products are often considered good sources of protein as well as many vitamins, minerals, and other essential nutritional benefits. Soybeans contain high amounts of protein, including all essential amino acids (the only such vegetable source with that distinction). Soybeans are also a rich source of calcium, iron, zinc, phosphorus, magnesium, B-vitamins, omega-3 fatty acids, and fiber. But Chapter 2 enumerated some of soy's dangers for babies, and bear in mind that soy has other dangers that go beyond infancy:

- Soybeans are acid-washed in factories at high temperatures and pressures in large and leaching aluminum tanks, with the help of a variety of chemicals. There is particular concern about very high levels of aluminum in soy products.
- Most of the farms where soybeans are grown use toxic pesticides and herbicides. Soy has one of the highest pesticide contamination levels of any crop.
- Soybeans are high in phytic acid, which is known to block the body's absorption of such minerals as calcium, zinc, magnesium, and iron.
- Soy contains isoflavones, plant hormones that mimic estrogen in the body. Some research has shown that isolated isoflavones, also known as phytoestrogens, contribute to the growth of tumors in the breast, endometrium, and uterus.

Can you give your family the benefits of soy without imparting its dangers? Yes.

- **Avoid non-organic soy ingredients.** In North America, all soy that is labeled "organic soy" is guaranteed to *not* be treated with herbicides.
- **Use soy products sparingly.** Occasional ingestion of traditionally processed soy products (miso, tempeh, tofu, soy milk) as part of a balanced, healthy diet should not create concern about

EATING OUT AS A VEGETARIAN

Many restaurants now offer vegetarian choices such as a salad bar, veggie burgers, pasta, vegetables, grains, and fruits. Mexican restaurants serve salsa, beans, rice, and vegetables. Thai menus always have a selection of vegetarian dishes such as spring rolls, soup, and noodle dishes like Pad Thai. You can easily find vegetarian sandwiches as well as soups in supermarkets and sandwich-oriented restaurants. Even fast-food places are getting in on it, offering such lower-fat choices such as salad bar, baked potatoes, and vegetarian chili.

soy. Eating miso soup several times per week and having tempeh or tofu in a dish a couple of times per week is fine.

- Rather than over-reliance on soy, use other legumes to get the bulk of your family's protein. Try incorporating into your diet various kinds of beans and bean products like hummus, made with chickpeas and often a surprise favorite with kids.

Why Vegetarianism Helps the Planet[10]

Eating a plant-based meal—rather than one based on meat, fish, eggs, or dairy products—is not only better for you, but it can have a big impact on the environment.

Everything that we eat—beef or barley, chicken or chickpeas, pork or peanut butter—comes from plants. We eat some of the plants directly—the barley, the chickpeas, the peanut butter—and we eat some of it converted by plant-eating animals into meat, eggs, and milk.

Animals, however, are inefficient at converting plants into meat, milk, and eggs. Relatively little of what *they* eat ends up in what *you* eat because animals use the food they ingest to keep themselves alive, to fuel their muscles so they can stand up, walk around, and keep their hearts beating and their brains working. The result is that it takes several pounds of corn and soy to produce one pound of beef, or one pound of eggs, one pound of milk, etc. That cow, pig, or chicken also has to eat a lot more protein, carbohydrates, and other nutrients than it yields in meat, eggs, or milk.

It takes enormous amounts of energy to transform food into less natural states. As an example, eating one peanut butter and jelly sandwich will save the equivalent of 2.5 pounds of carbon dioxide emissions over an average animal-based lunch like a hamburger, a tuna sandwich, grilled cheese sandwich, or chicken nuggets. That's about 40 percent of what you'd save driving around for the day in a hybrid instead of a standard sedan.

A peanut butter and jelly sandwich will also save about 280 gallons of water over the hamburger. To put this in perspective, three such sandwiches a month instead of three hamburgers will save about as much water as switching to a low-flow showerhead.

Additionally, a peanut butter and jelly sandwich will save twelve to fifty square feet of land from deforestation, over-grazing, and pesticide and fertilizer pollution.

So it's easy to see how eating meat, dairy, or eggs rather than plant foods not only uses a lot of diesel and gasoline to operate the machinery, pump the water for irrigation, and produce the chemicals, it also means the use of more land, water, and fertilizers and pesticides.

"What about fish?" you may ask. In our modern era, it takes a lot of fuel to catch fish. We catch about half our seafood, and because fishing boats use a ton of fuel, fishing produces a lot of carbon dioxide. Over-fishing waters can also impact our aquatic ecosystems. The other half of the seafood we consume is farmed, meaning that it causes the same problems as other animal products if those farmed fish eat grain and soy. If the farmed fish eat fish meal (made from wild-caught fish), that creates the same problems as those associated with wild-caught seafood: over-fishing and fuel-related greenhouse gas emissions.

THE "STONE AGE" POINT OF VIEW

Some nutritionists are looking into archeological evidence indicating that early human societies that were centered on a hunter-gatherer lifestyle experienced a high degree of health. It appears that our cave ancestors were slim, lean, fit, and healthy, and that they did not generally suffer from many of the chronic and degenerative diseases that plague us today, such as cancer, allergies, and heart disease. Given that the human genetic makeup is identical to what it was in the Stone Age, some scientists have noted that our ancestors were optimally adapted to the types of foods they could gather or hunt, and there's no evidence to suggest that modern humans are any different.

What was the original, natural diet for humans? Research into the human diet at a time before technology (and therefore before pollution and greenhouse gases were a consideration) has led to interest in a modern dietary regimen known as the *Paleolithic diet*. Popularly known as the "caveman diet," this nutritional plan is based on the presumed ancient diet of wild plants and animals that various human species habitually consumed before the advent of agriculture and the beginning of animal domestication, roughly 10,000 years ago.

Proponents of this diet argue that modern human populations subsisting on these "caveman" hunter-gatherer diets are largely free of the diseases of modern society.

The principle tenet of a Paleolithic diet is to eat only the foods that our ancestors could hunt or come upon in the wild, including meat, internal organs, chicken, and seafood as well as foods that could be gathered: eggs, insects, fruit, nuts (walnuts, brazil nuts, macadamia, almond), berries (strawberries, blueberries, raspberries), seeds, vegetables, mushrooms, herbs, and spices.

The diet eliminates foods that likely were rarely or never consumed by humans prior to 10,000 years ago. Potatoes and legumes (peas, beans, and peanuts) are excluded as are many breads and grains (cereal, pasta), as they require cooking or processing before consumption. Also, the diet avoids dairy products, salt, refined sugar, and processed oils.

It makes sense that a diet high in post-agricultural-era foods could be detrimental to our health. Because these foods are foreign to our bodies, our genes have not had the time or the evolutionary pressures to adapt to these new foods. The simplest approach to this diet is to ask yourself, "Would this food be edible in the wild, in the absence of technology?"

Those families that do not adopt a totally vegetarian lifestyle might be interested in this Paleolithic diet as a way to avoid the modern high-carbohydrate, high-fat, cereal-based diet full of nutrient-stripped products that have serious ramifications for our health. If you are considering the Paleolithic diet for your family, there are many sources of information available due to increasing popularity and potential health benefits.

Now you know . . .

A balanced diet is a child's best defense against illness. It is best to serve your family a variety of fresh, organic fruits, vegetables, and nuts while minimizing consumption of processed and prepared foods. Once children are completely attached to unhealthy foods, it's challenging to switch them over to healthier eating, so starting your kids early on good, healthy eating habits will go a long way toward overall health and happiness for your entire family.

FOOTNOTES

1. *The Wall Street Journal*, March 10, 2004.
2. *Pediatrics*, January 2010, Vol. 125, Issue. 1, 50–59 (doi:10.1542/peds.2009-0813).
3. Zuguo, Mei, Cynthia L. Ogden, Katherine M. Flegal, and Laurence M. Grummer-Strawn, "Comparison of the Prevalence of Shortness, Underweight, and Overweight among U.S. Children Aged 0 to 59 Months by Using the CDC 2000 and the WHO 2006 Growth Charts," *The Journal of Pediatrics*, November 2008,Vol. 153, Issue 5, 622–628.

4. World Health Organization and the Food and Agriculture Organization, Joint WHO/FAO Expert Consultation on Diet, Nutrition and the Prevention of Chronic Diseases (2002: Geneva, Switzerland).

5. Catorna, M.T., Y. Zhu, M. Froicu, et al., "Vitamin D status, 1,25-dihydroxyvitamin D3, and the immune system," *Am J Clin Nutr.*, 2004, Vol. 80 (Suppl):1717S–1720S, and Pittas A.G., J. Lau, F.B. Hu, et al., "Review: the role of vitamin D and calcium in type 2 diabetes. A systematic review and meta-analysis," *J Clin Endocrinol Metab.*, 2007, Vol. 92, 2017–2029.

6. Dietary supplements fact sheet: Vitamin D. National Institutes of Health dietary supplements. Available at: http://dietarysupplements.info.nih.gov/factsheets/vitamind.asp#h2. Accessed November 6, 2007.

7. "Infant Formula Supplementation With Long-chain Polyunsaturated Fatty Acids Has No Effect on Bayley Developmental Scores at 18 Months of Age-IPD Meta-Analysis of 4 Large Clinical Trials," *J Pediatr Gastroenterol Nutr.*, October 29, 2009.

8. "Position of the American Dietetic Association: Vegetarian Diets," *J. Am. Diet Assoc.*, July 2009, Vol. 109, Issue 7, 1266–1282.

9. News release, "PCRM Physicians Committee for Responsible Medicine Doctors Endorse Vegan and Vegetarian Diets for Healthy Pregnancies," March 2, 2009.

10. Reprinted with permission from *The PB&J Campaign* (www.pbjcampaign.org) The PB&J Campaign is an effort of private citizens concerned about the environment.

EMOTIONS

"Feelings of worth can flourish only in an
atmosphere where individual differences
are appreciated, mistakes are tolerated,
communication is open, and rules are flexible—
the kind of atmosphere that is found
in a nurturing family."

—Virginia Satir

6

The Good-Enough Mother: Transition

"I once risked the remark 'There is no such thing as a baby,' meaning that if you set out to describe a baby, you are describing a baby and someone. A baby cannot exist alone but is essentially part of a relationship."

—DONALD WINNICOTT

THE HUMAN RACE would not have survived if mothers had not met the infant's most basic needs. The connection between mother and baby is physiologically and psychologically designed to extend after birth.

The term "good-enough mother" has a specific psychological connotation as originated by Dr. Donald Winnicott, the mid-twentieth century pediatrician and psychoanalyst quoted above, who was describing what he considered to be optimal mothering.

According to Winnicott, "The 'good-enough mother' starts off with an almost complete adaptation to her infant's needs, and as time proceeds she adapts less completely..."

This mother is preoccupied during the first weeks of the baby's life, learning about and responding to the baby's all-encompassing needs. As the baby gets older, the good-enough mother intuitively recognizes both that the child can tolerate more frustration and that the child wants to exercise curiosity and do more things independently. As the mother lets the baby gradually separate, the baby gains more confidence to explore the environment and relate to others.

Because the mother, as time goes on, is not meeting her baby's demands immediately, the thinking is that rather than performing her duties "too well" or "too soon" she is taking a step back from that and responding in a way that's well *enough* and soon *enough*, thus allowing the child to soothe himself and come up with his own strategies for dealing with his frustration, thus becoming more independent from his mother. In Winnicott's terms, if the mother is "good enough," the child's needs are met *enough* of the time. The child is not distressed and does not feel overwhelmed. This gradual process also enables children to tolerate, rather than fear, feeling "negative" emotions.

Newborns and infants, being completely dependent, need their mother to satisfy *all* their needs as quickly as possible. As noted in previous chapters, you cannot "spoil" your newborn by picking him up too much, co-sleeping with him, or doing some of the other things that will build the mother-child bond. However, as your child gets older, if you try to satisfy all of his needs immediately, you'll prevent him from developing in healthy and important ways, as well as hindering him from learning to solve his own problems.

> The good-enough *mother* provides a safe haven to protect and comfort her child, as well as a secure base from which the child can grow and learn.

We should not confuse good enough with "merely good," which would be the popular connotation not rooted in psychobiology. That would suggest a mother who makes mistakes but is adequate. In

Winnicott's concept, the mother is not seen by the infant as good or bad but is perceived as a presence attuned to him over time.

The *good-enough* mother provides a safe haven to protect and comfort her child, as well as a secure base from which the child can grow and learn.

By not jumping immediately when your child needs something, he will eventually learn to:

- Wait
- Eat and get dressed independently
- Accept temporary separation when you're not there
- Tolerate frustration and continue trying to do something that is challenging
- Experience and deal with other negative feelings, like disappointment and sadness

Through her emotionally available but non-intrusive parenting, the mother lays the foundation for the *good-enough* toddler, who, in experiencing what it feels like for his mother to sometimes say "no," begins to understand that frustration and disappointment are normal, manageable, and tolerable aspects of life.

Transition

Winnicott's good-enough mother is one who caters to a child's every need early on in development and then gradually becomes less responsive as the child grows. This withdrawal helps the child adjust to the real world.

Winnicott further developed this idea in his discussion of the *transitional experience*. The child gradually goes through a period of separation from the mother. To ease the transition, the child typically becomes attached to the "transitional object"—a term first used by Winnicott to refer to inanimate objects, such as a soft toy or blanket, specially used to provide comfort or solace in infancy and early childhood.[1] The young child associates the transitional object with the comforting attention of the parent. Separation is less difficult

ENCOURAGING TRANSITIONAL OBJECTS

The transitional object should be offered *consistently* at *all times* whenever the baby is:

- Learning to sleep alone or without breast-feeding during the night
- In an unfamiliar place
- Is sad, lonely, or hurt
- Is afraid, upset, or stressed

for a child who can hold on to an inanimate object provided by the mother. The child carries this *lovey* or *blankey* everywhere, and essentially loves *it*. The transitional object is particularly important for the child at bedtime and as a defense at other anxious times. Winnicott stresses that these objects are a normal and significant part of a child's development.

Attachment to the transitional object can happen quite organically when a child shows an affinity for a particular object, or it may be encouraged by the mother or father who consistently offers a particular toy or blanket at bedtime and any time that that the child doesn't feel safe.

Attachment to a transitional object tends to develop around six months of age. This is when the first evidence of independence develops, but the attachment peaks when the child is about two-and-a half. This may be because between the ages of 2 and 3 children develop the necessary skills that allow them to emotionally relate to people other than those who are closest to them.

Some babies maintain this attachment through the preschool years and beyond. There is no predetermined time for abandonment of a transitional object. Your child will put it aside when he's ready. Most children outgrow the need and use the object less and less over time.

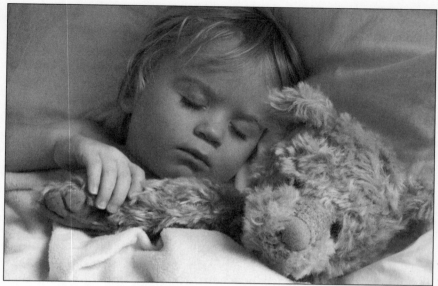

A soft toy or blanket provides comfort or solace in infancy and early childhood.

Responding Throughout the Stages of Childhood

The concept of *good-enough* could extend all through childhood.

As children become more aware of themselves as separate beings they want to assert themselves and have some control over their lives. At the same time, they look up to adults they trust as the strong and powerful beings who can take their pains and worries away when they're stressed and anxious.

At each stage, try to achieve a balance, where there's an emotional safety net for your child but also opportunity for choice and independence. Between the extremes of overbearing and negligent there's enough middle ground to find a path that suits your parenting style. Your job is to:

- Provide love and support
- Encourage exploration and curiosity
- Teach skills
- Allow the child to make appropriate choices

Sometimes exploration and the desire to do things independently takes young children into situations that require an adult's guidance when (for instance) choices are not safe or a task leads to a frustrating outcome. The *good-enough parent* learns over time when to step in and when to step back.

Toddlers can build a sense of competence by picking which book to read, which song to sing, or which hat to wear.

Preschoolers can do puzzles, put away toys, and learn how to dress themselves.

School-age children can feel responsible by cleaning up spills and doing chores, taking the school bus, choosing new friends, and helping parents begin to care for siblings or other family members.

Now you know . . .

By maintaining a balance between firm rules and honoring their child's choices whenever possible, a good-enough parent helps prepare her child for a healthy, independent life.

Footnote

1. Winnicott, D.W., "Transitional objects and transitional phenomena; a study of the first not-me possession," *Int J Psychoanal*, 1953, Vol. 34, Issue 2, 89–97.

7

Communication: Learning to Talk, Learning to Listen

"The most basic and powerful way to connect to another person is to listen. Just listen. Perhaps the most important thing we ever give each other is our attention...A loving silence often has far more power to heal and to connect than the most well-intentioned words."
—RACHEL NAOMI REMEN

Learning to Talk

Every time you bring your child to the doctor for a well visit, your pediatrician should be assessing your child's speech and language by talking to your child as well as by talking with you about what you've been noticing about your child's language development. And so much is going on, especially during the first two years. For example, even before first words appear between the ages of 12 to 15 months, infants typically smile, laugh, gurgle, babble, point at desired objects, enjoy looking at pictures and manipulating toys, and begin recognizing some spoken words. In addition, very young infants can begin imitating facial expressions and body gestures.

Although signs of communication delay are worrisome, many children are simply what we call "late talkers." These children typically have normal hearing, can comprehend spoken language, and can understand and respond to age-appropriate commands and questions, such as "We're going outside, so let's get your shoes," or "Do you want some water?" It may be easy for you to forget sometimes that even if your child isn't talking, or talking a lot, he may well understand much of what you're saying. Also, children who are late talkers have normal nonverbal problem-solving skills, which you'll see firsthand when your child starts assembling age-appropriate puzzles.

It is usually after the age of 24 to 30 months that the late talker will begin to show signs of "catching up."

Sign Language and Language Development

Children with normal hearing who learn sign language are able to communicate at a much earlier age than children who use spoken language alone.

Sign language helps hearing infants communicate because babies have control over their hands long before they develop the fine motor skills required for speech. Signing enables them to express what they are not yet able to say. By introducing simple signs that communicate specific needs, such as *nurse*, *milk*, and *more*, you can help make your young child's ability to communicate with adults less frustrating.

Learning sign language also helps children improve their language learning and IQs and actually accelerates a child's verbal language skills.

Psychologists Linda Acredolo and Susan Goodwyn, co-founders of the Baby Signs Institute, conducted a long-term National Institutes of Health-funded study[1] of 140 families. The goal of the study was to see if having parents teach sign language to their babies before they could talk helped their language development. The results were surprising. Babies taught to sign at eleven months who were later tested at the age of 3 were eleven months more advanced in their vocabulary and linguistic abilities than the babies who were not taught to sign (the control group). At age 8, signing babies scored higher on IQ tests than the control group.

It's never too early or too late to begin signing with your child. The optimum age to begin is at six or seven months. As you get into the habit of signing throughout the day you will start to notice your baby attempting to sign back to you. Find times throughout the day when the baby seems most receptive and repeat the sign often as you say the word verbally.

While you do not have to be fluent in American Sign Language (ASL) to teach your baby to communicate in this way, ASL is easy to learn because many of the signs mimic the idea that you are trying to convey. Start with four or five signs that relate to any part of your daily routine, and then introduce your child to new signs gradually. As with any language, repetition and praise are the keys to successful learning.

Television

Intense marketing for TV shows and DVDs created for young children could easily lead parents to believe that watching educational programming will stimulate their infants' brains and actually promote learning.

No study has ever shown that babies benefit from watching television and videos. Underscoring this lack of evidence was the decision by the Walt Disney Company in October 2009 to offer refunds to millions of parents who purchased its best-selling *Baby Einstein* learning videos. Disney was being threatened with a class-action lawsuit in which parents basically claimed that the videos were not making

> *No study has ever shown that babies benefit from watching television and videos. Just as there's no research to back up the claim that educational TV and videos are beneficial, there are multiple studies showing that television viewing is potentially harmful for very young children.*

their kids any smarter, and the refunds were seen as an apparent admission by the company that these videos do not boost infants' intelligence.

Just as there's no research to back up the claim that educational TV and videos are beneficial, there are multiple studies showing that television viewing is potentially harmful for very young children and that parents who buy educational DVDs to give their toddlers a head start may be doing more harm than good. One study suggests that television viewing tends to decrease babies' likelihood of learning language: babies who spent a lot of time sitting in front of a TV screen had inferior social, cognitive, and language skills by age 3 compared to babies who watched less television.[2] Another study by Washington University[3] found that for every hour that infants aged eight to sixteen months watch educational videos, they understood six to eight *fewer* words than babies not exposed to such videos. The University specifically mentioned *Baby Einstein* when announcing the study.

As your toddler's brain grows and develops, TV watching is the last thing he needs. Children learn by interacting with their environment: exploring, moving, playing, and socializing. Your common sense as a parent will tell you that your child will not learn from passively sitting in front of a box. Talking, singing, reading, listening to music, or playing are far more important to your child's development than any TV show.

In December of 2006 the American Academy of Pediatrics prepared a script for local print and broadcast media, and for school and community newsletters. This is what it said:

> It may be tempting to put your infant or toddler in front of the television, especially to watch shows created just for children under age 2. Resist the urge: the American Academy of Pediatrics says children under 2 should not watch TV of any kind because of how it can adversely affect your child's development. Pediatricians also strongly oppose targeted programming for young children, especially when it's used to market toys, games, dolls, unhealthy food, and other products.

FRANCE BANS BABY TV

The government of France has actually banned baby television. In a report published in July 2008, French researchers found that for children younger than 3, watching television undermined their development, encouraged passivity, delayed language acquisition, increased agitation, reduced concentration, and increased the incidence of sleep disorders. That same month, the French broadcasting authority *Conseil Superior Audiovisuel* (CSA) banned TV channels from marketing shows aimed at toddlers and ruled that cable programs for the very young must come with the stark warning: "Watching television can slow the development of children under 3, even when it is aimed specifically at them."

Learning to Listen to Children

Children are very aware of adult communication, both verbal and nonverbal. From the time that they are very young, they can tell when adults are not listening, or preoccupied but pretending to listen. Even when you think that you are listening, you might be just focusing on the words but not the meaning as you go about your business in an absent-minded way.

Children tune out when they don't like the tone, lecturing, or lack of listening in a conversation. If they think their part of the conversation is being ignored or rejected, they become angry or lose interest.

Do you know how you come across to your child? What is it actually like to talk to you? Are you encouraging or discouraging? Are you patient or impatient? Does the expression on your face show interest and respect, or indifference and distraction? Most of us have no idea how we really come across to our children.

Best tip: Try to avoid the posture many people effect in a conversation, which is looking like you're listening but you are really just

iStock

Being an effective listener requires skill and commitment. You need to listen with empathy and for meaning, and making solid eye contact reinforces to your child that you're focusing your attention on her.

planning what you are going to say next. If you're "plotting your next move"—listening only *with the intention of replying*—it's not only ineffective, but your child will pick up on it.

Effective Listening

Effective listening requires listening on an entirely different level. It is listening with empathy *and* listening for meaning. It involves trying to understand what the child is saying from his perspective rather than filtering it through your own experiences. It is related to the concept of "seeing through the eyes of your child."

Being an effective listener requires personal integrity, skill, and commitment, *which means that you must stop trying to evaluate, judge, or plan a reply while your child is speaking*. Rather, listen empathetically and then somehow indicate—through your eye contact, body language, or reflective listening (repeating back some of what you're hearing)—that you're listening.

How to Show You're Listening

- **Eye contact.** Focus! Look directly at your child as he's speaking, not off to one side. And don't continue doing something else while he's talking. Stop whatever else you're doing. Face your child squarely with your body to physically reinforce that he's the center of attention.

- **Listening without interrupting.** Does your body language acknowledge that you are listening? Use smiles, nods, and expressions of understanding to communicate to your child that you are listening. It is not necessary that you agree or disagree during this time—it's more important that your child knows that his words are being respected.

> The simple truth is that at any given moment in your life there will be distractions, problems, worries, and issues that will seem much more important and compelling than anything that your child is likely to say. You must consciously lay those matters aside and take charge of where your mind is focused.

- **Reflective listening.** Reflective listening involves hearing the feelings and meanings of your child while he's talking. It is a re-statement (in different words) of what your child is saying to you. You, in essence, mirror the words of your child and rephrase them back, checking for accuracy of understanding. Practice this technique: there can be a fine line between reflectively listening and interrupting. Done right, reflective listening provides positive affirmation, indicates your respect, and shows your child that you understand his message.

You must consciously choose to listen and to be emotionally present. The simple truth is that at any given moment in your life there will be distractions, problems, worries, and issues that will seem much more important and compelling than anything that your child is likely to say.

You must consciously lay those matters aside and take charge of where your mind is focused. Listen to your child the way that you would like to be listened to: with honesty, integrity, respect, and fairness.

Teach Children How to Listen

Have you ever made one of these statements?

- My child simply refuses to listen. The more I get upset, the worse he gets.
- He refuses to follow basic rules of behavior, ignores me, and screams when he doesn't get his way.
- I get so angry that I find myself yelling and can't seem to stop.
- "Why? Why doesn't he *listen?*"

Nobody likes to talk to someone who isn't listening—that goes for both children and adults. So you must learn how to be a good listener in order to teach your child how to listen to you.

Listening is a behavior that, fittingly, you can't teach by talking about it. Rather, listening is learned by observing and experiencing it. Chances are many of us never really learned how to listen, so it can be difficult to show children how.

If your child has learned—through watching you—that it's okay not to listen and to ignore your requests, then this pattern will happen again and again.

Besides you becoming a good listener yourself, there are other factors in teaching your child to listen to you. As mentioned, your physical presence and posture matter. For starters, you should try to be in the same room when trying to communicate with your child; you're likely to find that calling out questions or commands from the next room is seldom effective. While you're talking, your child's more apt to listen if you focus on him directly and authoritatively. You might find it helpful to physically get down to your child's level if he's at a table or sitting on the floor. Your body language must indicate that you are right there and engaged. With this approach your child will be much more likely to listen to what you have to say.

Anger

Sometimes, despite the internal awareness of loving our children, we behave in ways that do not display that love.

As hard as it may be for you to believe, there are times when you're going to feel very angry with your child. And when parents become angry, they often ascribe motives to children that do not exist, such as "He is doing this to get me" or "He's not happy unless I get mad," when in fact, children, especially young children, seldom have the deliberate intention of making their parents angry.

If you're angry at or around your child a lot of the time, it's critical that you bear in mind that your anger is not about your child. You may be feeling stressed about something that's going wrong in your life that is suddenly exacerbated by your child's behavior. Your anger does not make you a bad parent or indicate that something's wrong with you. Feeling depressed, guilty, disappointed, frustrated, useless, or just plain old tired can contribute to your anger.

Anger can often lead to yelling, a learned behavior from the parent's own experience of being yelled at as a child. As much as they regret it later, there are times during frustration or anger than parents lose control and blow up at their kids. However, make no mistake that yelling frightens children. Being yelled at makes children want to fight back or run away. They feel helpless.

Recognize that your child's "misbehavior" or "attacking you" is really a call for help—perhaps something you did or something that happened in their lives is making them feel fearful or unsafe. Then, instead of responding by yelling and perpetuating a negative pattern of communication, train yourself to respond calmly.

Being yelled at makes children feel helpless.

Fotolia

JUNK PRAISE

Building up your child's self-esteem does not call for constant praise and compliments. Undeserved praise is not authentic communication. Responding to your child's efforts thoughtfully and honestly is the basis for building self-esteem and helping him create the confidence he needs in meeting life's challenges.

Ways to handle your anger are as follows:

- Understand that there is almost always an underlying feeling having nothing to do with your child that is causing your anger; try to understand that feeling and root out its cause.
- It can be very damaging for children to be in a home where there is a lot of anger, *even if the anger is not directed at them.*
- If you feel angry, remove yourself from the situation; take a break until you can manage your feelings.

Hold Your Applause

Parents understandably praise their children for doing well because they want them to feel good about themselves. The problem with praise is that you can overdo it.

While there's nothing wrong with helping your child to feel a sense of pride, that feeling of satisfaction should be attached to a genuine achievement. If children are constantly praised for minimal effort or mediocre results, the words of praise, rather than the desire to learn and improve, become the ultimate goal. Your child becomes focused on pleasing you rather than becoming involved in the intrinsic pleasure of the activity.

Overdoing praise has long-term consequences. If your child's confidence is not built on his abilities and achievements, it could be devastating when your child gets into the "real world," such as school, and finds that his teachers have expectations of real performance.

This doesn't mean that you should discourage your child; just be strategic with your encouragement. Also be specific, especially when your child is very young. Emphasize his effort as well as specific characteristics of what your child may have done, whether it's a crayon drawing or his exemplary behavior at the dinner table.

Be Present

Another way to show encouragement is, quite simply, to be with your child. Just being in the same room can communicate to your child that you are interested and available, which is sometimes all he needs.

The Communication Pay-off

Being a skillful communicator requires patience, understanding, time, and space.

Your learning how to listen well and respect other people's autonomy and feelings—and showing your child how it's done—will lay the foundation for emotionally healthy relationships—including the one between you and your child—throughout his life.

Now you know . . .

While your child is learning to talk you must be learning (or re-learning) how to listen—a skill that takes a lot of practice, especially if you're going to pass it on to your child.

FOOTNOTES

1. Acredolo, L.P. and S.W. Goodwyn, "The long-term impact of symbolic gesturing during infancy on IQ at age 8," July 2000, Paper presented at the meetings of the International Society for Infant Studies, Brighton, UK.
2. "Television Viewing in Infancy and Child Cognition at 3 Years of Age in a U.S. Cohort," *Pediatrics*, March 2009, Vol. 123, Issue 3, e370–e375 (doi:10.1542/peds.2008-3221).

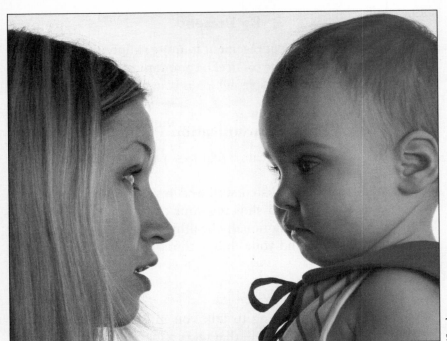

8

Discipline

("Treat Me Like I'm Someone You Love")

"The truth is, no matter how trying they become, babies two and under don't have the ability to make moral choices, so they can't be bad. That category only exists in the adult mind."
—ANNE CASSIDY

"Your children will become what you are; so be what you want them to be."
—DAVID BLY

"If there is to be peace in the world we must begin with the children."
—GANDHI

CHILDREN COME INTO THIS WORLD ready to learn, love, and play. They are emotionally pure, loving, and trusting. When they go on to behave in ways that we think are wrong, they are not intentionally being bad. They're just learning and exploring.

Discipline is from a Latin word "discipulus," which means "learner." That makes you as the parent the "teacher"—your child needs your help in learning how to behave.

Guiding your child's behavior is challenging work, but it's your most important job as a parent. Discipline helps your child develop self-control, so eventually your child will possess the ability to guide his behavior and actions in proper ways in all situations, even when you're not there.

> It is not your job to make your child happy; it is your job to teach your child appropriate behavior that will potentially foster his happiness.

Through all the stages of their development, children need to know what's expected of them, which behaviors are acceptable and which are not. By making these expectations and behaviors clear, by giving approval and withholding approval, you're serving as a necessary authority figure for your child. This is not the same as being an authoritarian parent, who is demanding, controlling, inflexible, and distant. A parent of authority, while firm, is caring and kind.

It is not your job to make your child happy; it *is* your job to teach your child appropriate behavior that will potentially foster his happiness. Don't hesitate to say "no" for fear of upsetting your child. Children want the security of having somebody in charge.

Babies, the First Year

At around nine months, your baby is entering the age of independence, no longer completely in need of his mother for mobility and nourishment. It's not too early to begin teaching the basic rules about behavior. Even at such a young age, babies respond to their parents' approval and are encouraged to continue the behavior that elicits that approval. For instance, when parents delight in a baby's first word, the child is likely to continue to repeat the word many times over.

A nine-month-old is beginning to understand what you say as well as the nuances of your facial expressions and tone of voice. Because they don't understand much language yet, your demeanor, including how you say things, might well be more important at this stage than what you're actually saying. This goes for dangerous situations, too: your immediate, strong reaction with a raised voice—"Stop!" when your child is running into the street, for example—will get your child's attention even if he doesn't understand the word. Needless to say, you should probably try to reserve your alarming tone for such emergencies.

Your Baby, Year Two

Year two sees your bundle of joy shifting further away from that time where every little whimper was responded to patiently, all was calm, and love was all around.

At this age your child is becoming independent and learning about the world. Parents are often surprised that their child "knows what he wants" or "has a mind of his own." This is normal. Kids this age need to explore, run, climb, and touch, and as before are never deliberately "misbehaving." Know when to give in and when to be firm so that your child learns what's acceptable and what isn't.

Two-year-olds need your help in knowing how to act and how to manage their feelings. Say "no" when you need to and try to direct the child's interest elsewhere, essentially finding ways to turn that no into a "yes." And remember to praise the good things that your child does.

It's common for kids this age to kick, hit, and bite other children out of anger and frustration because they don't have the words to let those other people know that they're upset. If your child acts this way, the first thing to do is remove your child from the situation.

Tenacious Toddlers

The twos can be terrific as well as challenging. Just weeks ago it seems you were adept at distracting your child. Now you have a tenacious toddler, intent on demands that are no longer easily met. Your child's persistence will create conflict between the two of you and within yourself. How do you respond? Do you cave in? If you ignore demands, are you being too strict?

Most toddlers go through the "tantrums in the supermarket" or so-called "terrible twos" stage at about 2½ years, some as early as 18 months, some after. Your child will seem to delight in doing just what you don't want him to do. He'll demand things he shouldn't have or that he doesn't even want. His favorite word will be "no" even when he means "yes." It's a way for him to feel independent from you. His defiance also points to the conflict between wanting to explore the world while at the same time feeling frightened by all of his choices or frustrated by your rules. When your child reaches this stage, what will seem like misbehaving is really just growing up.

If you're having frequent struggles with your toddler, you're not alone. Just be firm and remember that on the day you can listen to your child cry, whine, stomp, kick, groan, and argue over something he wants without your giving in, you have grown as a parent.

Of course, if your child's behavior is harmful to himself or to others, you need to curb it immediately through your words or body language. It is up to you to keep your child safe and to teach your child how to avoid getting hurt. You must make a decision and stick with it when it involves an unsafe situation. And while you need to keep your child safe and teach him how to avoid getting hurt, don't prolong the negative attention during non-emergent situations: childish but harmless behavior that is ignored is less likely to continue.

Tantrums

Ask a toddler to do something that seems to him to be the direct opposite of what he wants, and his behavior can often rapidly deteriorate into a tantrum, a sudden explosion that appears out of proportion to the event that triggered it.

For the parent, tantrums can be alarming, frustrating and, when they occur in public, excruciatingly embarrassing. And if you think they're difficult for you, for the child they can be frightening and overwhelming. In that moment the child feels out of control, emotionally and physically, and he'll be unable to respond to reason, so don't even try.

When a child throws a tantrum, she feels out of control at that moment. She is likely frightened and cannot respond to reason.

iStock

Temper tantrums might be due to many things:

- Difficulty communicating
  - Your child can't understand what you are saying.
  - Your child can't express himself well enough to be understood.
  - Your child wants to do more than he's allowed and can't express his anger verbally.
- A physical problem
  - Your child may be hungry, tired, or anxious.
- Not yet being capable
  - Your child might not yet be adept at doing the things that he wants to do.

When your child is having a tantrum, as long as there is no danger to your child or others, you can:

- Ignore your child
- Distract your child
- Hug your child

Keep calm and be understanding. Never punish your child for having a tantrum. It helps to remember that tantrums are a normal part of growing up.

Even at a young age, babies respond to their parents' approval.

Be Positive When Appropriate

- When your child's desires are not really a big deal, unreasonable, or inappropriate—wanting to hold that balloon all day, for instance—there is no harm in giving in.
- Let the child make a decision within the larger context of the desired behavior. For instance, at lunchtime, you can ask, "Do you want soup or spaghetti?" and by allowing a choice, lunch is enjoyed without a struggle.
- Expressing encouragement when reasonable expectations are met and ignoring childish but harmless behavior are keys to helping your toddler through this stage of uncertainty.

By concentrating on the positive and backing off when appropriate during this phase of parenthood, you'll find that children at this age can really be fun. They say and do cute things and delight in the everyday awareness of things around them, which you'll appreciate as you view the world through their eyes.

Consistency Is the Key

By being consistent, you can teach appropriate behavior. In contrast, if your reactions are inconsistent, your child will never learn the desired behavior and this will only lead to frustration on both of your parts as you feel thwarted and your child does things that you might interpret as "being out to get you," which is, of course, not the case.

It's also true that if "consistency" is practiced by the child instead of the parent (persistent whining or tantrums), parents will eventually be worn down and confused about why the child "doesn't listen." The problem will become that the child has "consistently" learned how to get his or her way.

"Treat Me Like I'm Someone You Love"

Refrain from doing something to negate the wonderful natural traits that your child was born with. Avoid squashing children's joy or projecting onto them a malicious intent regarding what they were doing. Most likely, they haven't a clue as to why you are getting upset with them. They just end up feeling bad by observing your tone of voice and facial expressions. This sets them up to think that something is wrong with them. You can help your children feel good about themselves by disciplining them without judging them.

> If you say that there are going to be consequences, it's important that you follow through. If not, you'll only be setting up a pattern of being ignored.

How can you be an effective disciplinarian? *Not by losing control and not by yelling*. It is frightening for a child when a parent is out of control. Speak to your child clearly and concisely, explaining in words that the child can understand that "this is not appropriate." If you say that there are going to be consequences, it's important that you follow through. If not, you'll only be setting up a pattern of being ignored.

In all your daily situations, clearly express to your child what constitutes acceptable behavior. If you need to reprimand your child at any age, do it privately. Respect his self-esteem and sense of worth by being kind but firm and help build that self-esteem by giving realistic praise. If you find yourself getting angry at your child, make a conscious decision to avoid attacking words that only leave a child feeling defensive and helpless. It is your own desire to change that will be the first step toward your child's more reasonable behavior.

Anxiety and Stress

Your child will experience anxiety as he begins to understand some of the realities of the world, which to him may be disappointing and sometimes frightening. From his point of view, the feeling of being afraid and out of control is probably a practical definition of anxiety. It is particularly common for your child to experience this kind of anxiety between the ages of 2 and 6.

Young children may have short-lived fears, such as fear of the dark, storms, or animals. Natural developmental fears during these years might include fear of being left alone and fear of strangers. Life transitions, such as the start of daycare, being away from home, moving to a new location, and separation from parents or caregivers are also stressful events for children.

Children may express stress differently according to their age, maturity level, and previous experiences. Pay attention to the following symptoms and behaviors in your child, all of which can be due to stress.

Young children react in these ways when the stability and security of their lives are violated. Don't confuse your child's occasional moment-to-moment inappropriate behavior with regressive behavior that may be a reaction to stress. Regressive behavior is a cry for help from a child who is not feeling safe or who feels unable to cope with his situation.

TODDLERS	PRESCHOOLERS	ELEMENTARY SCHOOL CHILDREN
regress to infant behaviors	anger	whining
feel sad	irritability	acting withdrawn
fear being alone	withdrawal	being distrustful
bite	anxiety	feeling unloved
be sensitive to loud or sudden noises	fear of being alone	worrying about the future
become angry or aggressive	regress to infant behaviors	complaints of head or stomachaches
	uncontrollable crying	loss of appetite
	eating problem	trouble sleeping
	sleep problems including nightmares	

It is important not to blame or punish these children, who are in particular need of being cared for and protected. Children under stress need help in expressing their feelings and concerns. Their fears need to be addressed because they are certainly real to the child.

Teaching Correct Behavior

Behavior is not taught to children by talking about it. Rather, correct behavior is demonstrated, observed, and experienced. Children learn kindness and compassion through watching you and other adults behaving kindly and sympathetically toward others. They learn to be nice by having someone be nice to them. They learn to be peaceful and non-violent by having other people demonstrate what it is to be peaceful.

Respect children as people. Teach kindness by being kind.

Now you know . . .

Babies and children must be treated with affection, consideration, courtesy, and dignity as you guide them toward appropriate behavior.

9

Attention

CHILDREN ARE NATURALLY ACTIVE, exuberant, easily distracted and, at times, very uncooperative. Almost all have times when they are out of control: in constant motion, making noise, crashing into everything around them and lacking the patience to wait their turn. At other times they may drift as if in a daydream, failing to pay attention or finish what they start.

Taken individually, impulsive, inattentive, and hyperactive behaviors are perfectly normal. However, for children diagnosed with Attention Deficit Disorder (ADD), or particularly Attention Deficit Disorder with Hyperactivity (ADHD), these behaviors are so constant, so disruptive, and so unmanageable that parents can't keep control, teachers can't teach, and the children themselves don't socialize well. An impulsive nature may put them in actual physical danger. In short, children with ADHD have behavior problems that are so frequent that they interfere with their ability to have normal lives.

Attention Deficit Disorders

These are children who:

- tune out in the middle of a conversation
- are disorganized
- appear lazy or unreliable
- chronically procrastinate
- get very impatient and easily frustrated
- act or speak impulsively
- interrupt others
- frequently feel restless or bored or carry on many projects at the same time
- have difficulty focusing on one thing at a time, unless it's a favorite activity such as playing video games
- are in constant motion—moving, roaming, squirming, talking, tapping feet
- have temper outbursts

Diagnosis

Deciding whether a child has those characteristics can be very subjective, so making an accurate diagnosis can be difficult. Attention deficit is a psychiatric diagnosis, not a medical one. There's no sign of physical abnormality in these children, and there is no test or scan to prove that it exists.

ADHD is a psychiatric behavioral disorder that manifests as a persistent pattern of inattention and/or hyperactivity-impulsivity that is more frequent and severe than is typically observed in individuals at a comparable level of development.

Professionals base their assessments solely on what they observe. It would be easy for someone who did not understand children and their basic natures to render a diagnosis of ADD/ADHD. The ideal assessment of a child for an attention disorder requires that a clinician talk with parents, teachers, and other people who interact with the child in varied settings. Yet children are most commonly diagnosed

by pediatricians who have only a few minutes during brief office visits to make the call. It is indeed a challenge for a pediatrician to determine which children are having difficulties appropriate for their
age and those whose behavior is truly pathological.

ADHD tends to run in families. For approximately half of the children affected by it, symptoms run into adulthood. In early childhood, boys are much more likely than girls to be diagnosed with it.

Causes

In recent years, scientists who study early-childhood development
have been taking a closer look at the part of the brain that is responsible for what are being called "executive functions." Originally
a neuroscience term, it refers to the ability to plan, organize, pay
attention to details and instructions, screen out irrelevant information, carry a plan through to completion, avoid distractions, process
information in a coherent way, hold relevant details in short-term
memory, and focus on the task at hand.

You might consider "executive functions" as the skills that help us
to manage our lives and be successful.

Cognitive psychologists have now come to believe that executive
functions, and specifically the skill of self-regulation, might hold the
answers to some of the difficulties exhibited by children who are
diagnosed with ADD and ADHD.

The executive functions occur in the area of the brain called the
prefrontal cortex (the very front of the brain, located right behind
the forehead). This is the newest part in evolutionary terms, and one
of the last regions to reach maturity during human development. As
you can imagine, impairment in this part of this brain leads to difficulties with attention span, memory, perseverance, judgment, organization, and impulse control.

Given that children diagnosed with ADD and ADHD have difficulties with executive functions, there is a growing body of research
to investigate the possibility of training the healthy development
of these functions, thereby reducing the likelihood of problem behaviors. Any training would likely be most effective during the pre-

school and early elementary years when this part of the brain is continuing to mature.

School and Learning

Consistent with ideas about executive function, it appears that children with ADD/ADHD have a different kind of intelligence. They are creative and curious. They like to observe and explore. They like to learn how things work and are drawn to things that are new or unexpected.

This is not the kind of academic ("executive") intelligence usually cultivated in school. Typical schoolwork revolves around focus and planning, setting goals and reaching objectives. Information is acquired and children take tests to prove that they have absorbed a specific set of skills and facts.

Children with ADD/ADHD are not good at planning and aiming for precise goals. In truth, it is not that they cannot pay attention, but they cannot *stop* paying attention: they are distracted because they have trouble focusing on just one event and shutting out all the rest.

Some children simply cannot adapt to the typical school environment, where they are expected to sit at a desk for hours at a time, work on a task within the time allowed, memorize everything that the teacher says, and be quiet so as not distract the rest of the class. They want to learn, but they exhibit strong unfavorable reactions to the classroom environment and become "fidgety." They are considered a disruption and an inconvenience—and are given the label of "a problem child."

Most public schools have a low tolerance for mild behavioral problems. Parents are often left to wonder, "Does my child actually have ADHD if the teacher says he does?"

Teachers are *not permitted* to diagnose ADHD. They are, however, allowed—indeed encouraged—to advise you that your child displays certain characteristics and that it would be advisable to have your child evaluated for ADHD by a healthcare professional. They are not permitted to mention the possible use of stimulant medication. They cannot, under any circumstances, suggest that your child is not welcome at the school unless he takes stimulant medication.

Some children simply cannot sit at a desk for hours at a time. When they stop concentrating on their homework and become fidgety, allow them time to explore and play in a natural environment; this lets them use their imagination and also helps them with their attention difficulties.

Junk Play vs. Real Play

Technology is one of the first things to look at when dealing with a child who demonstrates attention problems or hyperactivity: children who have difficulty paying attention in school can sit for hours in front of video and computer games. A child who regularly plays these games is being exposed to constantly and rapidly changing stimuli, to which he becomes quickly conditioned. These games require quick reaction and skill but not logical thinking or planning ahead. Television is equally detrimental. The constant stream of loud noises, bright colors, and changing camera angles contributes to short attention span. After much exposure to these devices, children cannot sit still or focus. These children would be calmer if they spent more time playing outdoors in natural surroundings.

The modern experience of childhood is radically different than in past generations, when children learned about the natural world on farms, in neighborhood parks, and in families' gardens. They spent time exploring woods, creeks, ravines, swamps, and ponds.

Few contemporary children get a chance to walk or bike to school, camp under the stars, follow a trail, climb a tree, play hide and seek outdoors, or catch a fish. Schools emphasize more and more homework. Children are driven on superhighways to shopping malls. At home, parents tend to keep their children indoors because they fear having them exposed to traffic, strangers, and sunlight.

When children are not free to explore and play in natural environments, attention difficulties—as well as obesity and depression—are often a consequence.

Outdoor free play is important to children—climbing, running, building, and taking part in other unstructured whole-body activities—all the while using imagination fully. Playing helps children to manage stress and enjoy their natural exuberance.

Nutrition

Nutrition was discussed in Chapter 5, and is particularly important in children with attention disorders.

Food affects behavior, memory, and learning. Moreover, children have specific and complex nutritional needs that are not met with the standard American diet. Learning requires optimal health and brain function. If a child is eating the wrong foods or foods deficient in the proper nutrients, his learning ability will be compromised.

A typical American child's diet contains large amounts of over-processed, packaged foods with unnecessary, harmful ingredients. These foods are vitamin and mineral deficient and full of pesticides. Freezing, frying, and overcooking further compromise the vitamin content. Sugary donuts and cereal can affect a child's ability to pay attention and cause irritability. Artificial colors, flavors, and preservatives may also contribute to difficulty with thinking, coordination, and memory.

Certain ingredients and foods can quickly drain your child's energy and attention levels, often causing short spikes in activity followed by crashing lows spurred by excess sugar and artificial ingredients. Check labels and ingredient lists and steer clear of the following:

- Foods with artificial sweeteners or coloring
- High-fructose corn syrup
- Sugary fruit drinks, colas, and juices
- Refined white sugars and breads
- Trans fats/partially-hydrogenated oils
- Processed snack foods and luncheon meats

Instead, serve whole, organic foods—in which nothing has been added or lost in processing. These real foods supply natural vitamin and mineral content without harmful additives, and ensure optimal functioning.

As noted in the nutrition chapter, start good dietary habits early, because it's not easy to change your child's diet once he's attached to unhealthy foods. It takes time, persistence, and effort for you and your child, and usually the entire family needs to cooperate. If you're successful in changing everyone's diet, you'll see beneficial behavioral changes in your child and will improve the overall health and happiness of your entire family.

Brain Foods

Nutritional yeast has high levels of amino acids, which are important because they enhance communication between brain cells and are necessary for mental clarity, memory, and concentration. It is also an excellent source of protein and vitamins, especially the B-complex vitamins.

Lecithin, as noted in Chapter 5, promotes brain development and also boosts memory and concentration. Lecithin is found naturally in egg yolk, grains, fish, and other foods.

Omega-3 fatty acids, also as noted in Chapter 5, are known to help with brain and nervous system function. The omega-3 oils, which are found in significant amounts only in oily fish, make up a quarter of the gray matter of the brain and are vital to brain and eye development.

As mentioned in the nutrition chapter, ample levels of omega-3 fats are available in breast milk, and a form of omega-3 (DHA) is now

OMEGA-3 FISH OILS

- Research in Britain (the Durham Sure Start trial)[1] suggests that children who have diets poor in omega-3 fatty acids are not achieving their natural potential. This study showed dramatic improvement in the behavior of preschool children when they were given a daily dose of fish oils. Children were assessed for their motor skills, IQ, reading, spelling, and behavior. After just six weeks of daily doses of omega-3, parents reported significant changes in the behavior and learning abilities of children as young as 20 months old.
- In 2006, a BBC series, "Child of Our Time," showed how fish oils can calm disruptive children age 6 and upwards.
- A double blind study conducted by the University of Oxford (England), in which children were given omega-3 fatty acids, concluded that "significant improvements for active treatment versus placebo were found in reading, spelling, and behavior over three months of treatment…"[2] This study suggests that children with symptoms of ADHD may do as well by taking omega-3 fatty acid supplements as they do with prescription stimulant drugs.

added to infant formula for that reason, but this supplementation does not emulate the benefits of breast milk. Several studies have demonstrated that children with lower levels of omega-3 fatty acids in their bloodstream have significantly more behavioral problems, temper tantrums, and learning, health, and sleep problems than do those children with high proportions of those fatty acids.[3,4] Once they are no longer breast-feeding, children can take supplements of omega-3 oils in the form of fish oil capsules (250 milligrams of DHA for children 7 years and older) or the old-fashioned cod liver oil (one teaspoon per fifty pounds of body weight). Vegetarians can find DHA supplements derived from algae. Dietary sources of omega-3s are chicken, eggs, and beef—but only if the animals have been fed green plants or algae. Look for cage-free chickens and pasture-fed cattle. Small, cold-water fatty fish are a good source (sardines, salmon, herring) but larger fish from the ocean or fish farms might contain mercury or pesticides, so limit your consumption of tuna, swordfish, and shark.

Allergies and Environmental Illness

Some children who are considered to have hyperactivity or attention problems are actually suffering from food or environmental allergies. Cow's milk is one of the biggest culprits of allergies in children. It might be a good idea to remove all milk products from the child's diet for at least a month, reading labels very carefully for ingredients such as whey, casein, or cream. Other foods that can commonly cause allergies are wheat, corn, soy, eggs, citrus fruits, and peanuts. Additional things to look out for are nitrates (found in hot dogs, bacon, and luncheon meats), MSG, caffeine, artificial colors and preservatives, and any foods with hydrogenated or partially hydrogenated oils (trans fats). Read the labels: almost all packaged foods have some or all of the above ingredients.

Read labels carefully for hidden (disguised) ingredients.

iStock

Modifying Behavior

Both parents and teachers can do much to support and train their children to manage their frustrating and stressful weaknesses, by doing such things as:

- helping to keep track of what gets done and what doesn't;
- moving a child's desk closer to the teacher's;
- creating small steps toward solving problems so that a child feels mastery.

Activities such as karate classes, team sports, and dance and music lessons also may help a child develop focus.

Parent Training as a Behavioral Intervention

Parent skills training has been used for years to improve the behavior of children. Research has found that for children with ADHD, having parents who use effective parenting techniques is one of the best predictors of success in adulthood.

The parent training recommended is not specific to ADHD but rather teaches behavior management skills that could be used with all children. Parents are given suggestions for how to use praise and rewards for good behavior, and for helping children learn to focus.

In England, the British government has mandated parent training as the first choice for treatment of ADHD. In many cases, parents of such children are offered free government-funded classes in parenting techniques.

Medications

Medications are used to reduce the symptoms of hyperactivity, inattentiveness, and impulsivity in both children and adults with ADD or ADHD.

Stimulants are the most common type of medication prescribed for attention deficit disorder. The stimulant medications include

TIPS FOR TALKING TO ADD CHILDREN

- Set realistic goals and provide opportunity for success.
- Use clear, brief directions.
- Provide organizational help. Record important information in a notebook.
- Don't give instructions or ask a question unless you have a child's full attention.
- Don't yell or shout when addressing an ADHD child.
- Don't repeat the same command over and over rapidly. ADHD children have a delayed reaction time.
- Be very direct and specific in your requests.
- Be consistent in your expectations and requirements, as well as your discipline and praise.

widely-used drugs such as Ritalin and Adderall. Although it sounds counterintuitive to give stimulants to a person who is hyperactive, these drugs are thought to boost activity in the parts of the brain responsible for attention and self-control.

These stimulant medications are classified as *Schedule Two* drugs by the United States Drug Enforcement Agency, as are cocaine and morphine. Schedule Two includes drugs of addiction that can only be prescribed by a doctor. They must always be kept securely locked away. Prescriptions can only be written by hand, in thirty-day supply and presented to the pharmacist in person—they cannot be phoned in or faxed.

Although the pills may help improve the ability to concentrate, control impulses, and follow through with tasks, children with ADD / ADHD might still struggle with forgetfulness, emotional problems, and social awkwardness.

In February 2007, the FDA issued warnings about stimulant medication side effects such as growth stunting and psychosis, among other mental disorders. Having ADHD is itself a risk factor for other mental health problems, but the possibility also exists that stimulant

**MEDICATIONS PRECLUDE ENTRY
INTO THE U.S. MILITARY FORCES**

The current use of medications in order to assist in managing the symptoms of AD/HD is per se disqualifying even if the medication would effectively enable the applicant to adapt to military life.

Department of Defense Directive 6130.3 provides in part: *Current use of medication to improve or maintain academic skills (e.g., methlyphenidate hydrochloride) is disqualifying.*

---

treatment during childhood might contribute to these high rates of accompanying diagnoses.

The most recent and best-documented problem associated with the stimulants used to treat ADHD concerns the stunting of children's growth. In a 2007 analysis,[5] a National Institute of Mental Health study—Multimodal Treatment Study of Children with Attention Deficit Hyperactivity Disorder (MTA)—over three years compared growth rates of unmedicated 7- to 10-year-olds with those of children who took stimulants throughout that period. The drug-treated youths showed a decrease in growth rate, gaining, on average, two fewer centimeters in height during the three years, and they never caught up with their peers.

Another report from the same study showed stimulant drugs such as Ritalin provide *no long-term benefit* in the treatment of ADHD: the stimulant drugs improved the social functioning and reduced symptoms of inattention and hyperactivity in children with ADHD only during the first year of treatment. Researchers followed the several hundred children enrolled in the study for eight years and found that children who remained on medication for that entire time showed no improvement in symptoms over those who had stopped taking the drugs.

William E. Pelham, Jr., M.D., University at Buffalo Distinguished Professor of Psychology, Pediatrics, and Psychiatry and co-author of the MTA study, says that the study is consistent with a large body of literature that fails to find any evidence of beneficial effects of stimulant medications on ADHD children's long-term outcomes.

"If you put a child on medication, he or she is far better right at that time. The question for parents is: Is this going to make a benefit for my child long term?" says Dr. Pelham. "The answer is no. Behavioral treatments are going to have much better benefit in the long term."

It's important to learn the facts about medication for ADD/ADHD so you can make an informed decision about what's best for your child.

Medication Does Not Cure ADD

Even when medication is effective in relieving symptoms of ADD/ADHD, it only works on the day that the drug is being taken. It does not cure ADD/ADHD. When medication stops, those symptoms return.

Now you know . . .

Medication can help reduce the symptoms of hyperactivity, inattentiveness, and impulsivity in children with ADD/ADHD, but medications come with side effects and risks with no long-term benefits—and they're not the only treatment option. Attention issues can also be helped by changes in parenting—such as using praise and rewards for good behavior—as well as adapting an organic, whole foods diet to help your child function at his highest level of health.

FOOTNOTES

1. "The effect of diet on behaviour and learning—a Sure Start initiative," written by Dr. Madeleine Portwood, Specialist Senior Educational Psychologist, Durham Local Education Authority. http://childrenfirst2006.co.uk/the-effect-of-diet-on-behaviour-and-learning-a-sure-start-initi.html.

2. Richardson, Alexandra J. and Paul Montgomery, "The Oxford-Durham Study: A Randomized, Controlled Trial of Dietary Supplementation With Fatty Acids in Children With Developmental Coordination Disorder," *Pediatrics*, May 2005, Vol. 115, Issue 5, 1360–1366.

3. Stevens, L., et al., "EFA supplementation in children with inattention, hyperactivity, and other disruptive behaviors," *Lipids*, October 2003, Vol. 38, Issue 10, 1007–1021.

4. Mitchell, E.A., et al., "Clinical characteristics and serum essential fatty acid levels in hyperactive children," *Clinical Pediatrics*, August 1987, Vol. 26, 406–411.

5. *Journal of the American Academy of Child & Adolescent Psychiatry*, August 2007, Vol. 46, Issue 8, 1015–1027.

MAINTAINING HEALTH

"It's bizarre that the produce manager
is more important to my children's health
than the pediatrician."

—MERYL STREEP

10

The Sunshine Vitamin

WE TAKE IT TOTALLY FOR GRANTED, but natural light is as much a nutrient as food and water. If people are exposed to enough sunshine, they do not need vitamin D from foods, nor do they run the risk of excessive dosage of the vitamin. Sunlight is the best source of natural vitamin D and you should seek it out whenever possible, while taking steps to avoid sunburn, of course.

In a 2009 study[1], researchers who looked at data on more than 6,000 children across the United States found that 70 percent had disturbingly low vitamin D levels. This is because contemporary children spend so much time indoors. Even when outdoors, they often wear sunscreen, which health agencies and dermatologists have long advised are needed to prevent skin cancer. Now some scientists are questioning that advice, recognizing that lack of sun exposure is putting children at risk of heart disease, rickets, weak bones, weak immune systems, and certain types of cancer.[2]

> Sunlight is the best source of natural vitamin D and you should seek it out whenever possible.

But what if it isn't sunny? It may surprise you to learn that it isn't necessary to have year-round exposure to sunlight because it's possible to accumulate vitamin D in your tissues during seasons when you are exposed to high amounts of sunlight. When your body accumulates enough vitamin D it'll be stored and then used up slowly during the darker months. Vitamin D is fat soluble—meaning the vitamin will dissolve if exposed to fat—so it's important to have sufficient, good quality fats in your diet in order to sufficiently store vitamin D for the winter months.

While vitamin D can be obtained orally, an excess of supplemental vitamin D can be seriously toxic, causing calcification of soft tissues and of the walls of your blood vessels, heart tissues, and lungs. Natural exposure to sunlight is preferable, as your body will absorb the vitamin D it needs and no more, thereby avoiding any chance of toxicity.

Because vitamin D is necessary to absorb calcium from the small intestine, it's particularly important for your child to maintain optimum levels of the vitamin. All that is required is sun exposure (face, hands, and arms) at least twice a week for about ten to twenty minutes each day, depending on the person's skin, the season, the time of day, and your distance from the equator. The best time of day for sun exposure is 11 A.M. to 1 P.M., but avoid the midday sun in the summer to minimize the chance of sunburn. Most important is that your child spends this time in the sun without sunscreen, as it interferes with the production of vitamin D.

A sunscreen with SPF (Sun Protection Factor) of 8 gives you only 5 percent of your normal vitamin D production; any SPF higher than that ensures you get NONE.

Hazardous Chemicals

Aside from inhibiting your body's natural production of vitamin D, sunscreens may contain toxic chemical ingredients that are in turn carcinogenic, or cancer causing. Many of these sunscreens have never been safety tested or safety approved by the Food and Drug Administration. The sunscreen's ingredients get absorbed right through the skin (a porous organ that absorbs most substances with which it comes into contact) and enter the bloodstream.

In July 2008, the non-profit Environmental Working Group (EWG) began studying brand-name sunscreens for safety and effectiveness. In their 2009 review[3] of 1,572 sunscreen products, the EWG determined that three out of five sunscreens offer inadequate protection from the sun or contain ingredients with hazardous chemicals.

What about Skin Cancer?

Despite increased sunscreen usage, skin cancer rates have risen. It now appears that *many heavily-used chemical sunscreens may actually increase the likelihood of getting cancers* by virtue of their cell-damaging free radicals, which could initiate a reaction that may ultimately lead to melanoma and other skin cancers.

> Worldwide, the greatest rise in melanoma (the deadliest form of skin cancer) has been experienced in countries where chemical sunscreens have been heavily promoted.

Worldwide, the greatest rise in melanoma (the deadliest form of skin cancer) has been experienced in countries where chemical sunscreens have been heavily promoted.

Physical Sunblocks

More effective and safer than chemical sunblocks are physical sunblocks, whose active ingredients—zinc oxide and titanium dioxide—are naturally occurring minerals that protect against overexposure to UV rays and work as a physical barrier against sun damage. Zinc oxide and titanium dioxide are particularly valuable because of their ability to filter UVA (a part of the ultraviolet rays from the sun that penetrate most deeply into the skin, causing skin damage that can in turn lead to skin cancer) as well as UVB (a sunburn-causing portion of ultraviolet rays). In short, physical sunblock ingredients reflect and refract UV light before it can reach your skin's surface.

The SPF value on sunblock indicates its UVB protection level against sunburn, which can give a false sense of security because the protection allows for more time in the sun, therefore prolonging cancer-causing UVA exposure. Any sunscreen that you choose must have UVA as well as UVB protection.

Zinc oxide has been used by lifeguards for years. It is considered a very effective and safe sunscreen ingredient, and also has anti-inflammatory properties. Zinc oxide is actually the only FDA-approved sunscreen for use on children under six months of age. As it happens it is also the most common ingredient in diaper rash ointments.

> Zinc oxide is actually the only FDA-approved sunscreen for use on children under six months of age. As it happens it is also the most common ingredient in diaper rash ointments.

Historically, when used in sunscreens, zinc oxide and titanium dioxide were visible, giving the skin a white color. This effect can be reduced when these chemicals are used in *nanoparticle* form, where they cannot be seen on the skin but still retain the sun-screening properties of the coarser material. Nanomaterials can measure as little as perhaps one-10,000th the width of a human hair. Such sunscreen formulations are now readily available—they are non-whitening, they spread easily on the skin, and they are not greasy.

Nanoparticles

Recently there have been questions about the safety of sunscreens that contain nanoparticles. Concerns relate to the theoretical possibility that if nanoparticles were to be absorbed into skin cells, they could possibly interact with sunlight to increase the risk of damage to these cells.

According to a July 2009[4] report by the Australian government, it would appear that nanoparticles are safe:

- The potential for titanium dioxide and zinc oxide nanoparticles in sunscreens to cause adverse effects depends primarily upon

the ability of the nanoparticles to reach viable [living and grow-
ing] skin cells; and

- to date, the current weight of evidence suggests that titanium
  dioxide and zinc oxide nanoparticles do not reach viable skin
  cells; rather, they remain on the surface of the skin and in the
  outer layer of the skin that is composed of non-viable cells.

A more cautious report,[5] issued in August 2009 by a coalition
of groups, including Friends of the Earth and Consumers Union,
urged people to avoid sunscreens containing nano-forms of zinc oxide, saying their risks were unknown. Concern was also expressed
that little is known about whether substances engineered at the nano
scale persist and accumulate in the environment in unusual and potentially harmful ways.

The United States Environmental Protection Agency (EPA) is currently working to identify how nano-materials move in the environment, the problems they might cause for people, animals, and plants,
and how these problems could be avoided or mitigated.

On balance, it seems that the manufactured nano-scale zinc and
titanium oxides are not necessarily the safest choice for effective sun
protection. Some parents are selecting brands found in the health
food stores with particle sizes at or above 100nm, assuming that they
bring less theoretical risk; these brands cause only a slight lightening
of skin color while worn. If you'd rather not use the more opaque
metal-oxide based sunscreens (titanium oxide or zinc oxide), these
larger particle brands may be the best compromise available today
between the whiteness from the metal oxides and any potential problems with nanoparticles.

Vitamin D and Autism

As evidence of widespread vitamin D deficiency grows, some scientists are wondering whether a deficiency of this critical substance—
once considered only important in bone health—may actually play
a role in autism.

Photo Courtesy of Melody Indigo Markel

We need to look carefully at what we are doing now in the twenty-first century that may be harming our health and the health of our children.

The theory that vitamin D deficiency causes autism is plausible. For one thing, falling vitamin D levels due to sun-avoidance over the last two decades correlates with a rapid increase in autism during that same time. Autism is also more common in areas where exposure to natural sunlight is inhibited, such as regions with latitudes toward the poles, urban areas, areas with high air pollution, and areas of high precipitation.

A study published in November 2008 in *The Archives of Pediatrics & Adolescent Medicine*,[6] a publication of the Journal of the American Medical Association, suggested a link between autism and places that get higher than average rain. Researchers at Cornell University found that autism rates in counties in California, Oregon, and Washington were positively related to the amount of precipitation in those counties. "Autism prevalence was higher for [children] that experienced relatively heavy precipitation when they were younger than three years," the authors write in the study. "This corresponds to the time at which autism symptoms usually appear and when any post-natal environmental factors would be present."

Rainfall's effect on autism could be due to lack of exposure to sunshine. Alternatively, high levels of precipitation may lead to more time indoors and thus more indoor activities, such as television and video viewing, which affect behavioral and cognitive development. The increased amount of time spent indoors also may expose children to more harmful chemicals, such as those in cleaning products, or even from more indoor mold growth in more humid climates.

A link between autism and vitamin D deficiency may also be suggested by evidence that vitamin D affects brain development, so if the vitamin's level is low, that development could be impaired.

Before the sun-scare campaign was started by the American Medical Association in 1989, people were getting 90 percent of their vitamin D via sunlight exposure to their skin. Diet accounts for very little of the vitamin D circulating in blood and it's hard to get enough from food alone.

As we see the incidence of autism and autism spectrum disorders reach epidemic proportions, we need to look carefully at what we are doing now in the twenty-first century that may be harming our health and the health of our children.

While overexposure to the sun can be detrimental, denying your body sunlight's benefits can be even more problematic.

> While overexposure to the sun can be detrimental, denying your body sunlight's benefits can be even more problematic.

Now you know . . .

Sun exposure to the skin is the human race's intended, most effective, and most natural source of vitamin D.

FOOTNOTES

1. Kumar, "Prevalence and Associations of 25-Hydroxyvitamin D Deficiency in US Children: NHANES 2001–2004," *Pediatrics*, September 1, 2009, Vol. 124, Issue 3, e362–e370.

2. Holick, M.F., "Vitamin D deficiency," *N Engl J Med.*, 2007, Vol. 357, 266–281.

3. EWG 2009 Sunscreen Guide, 2009 report.

4. "A review of the scientific literature on the safety of nanoparticulate titanium dioxide or zinc oxide in sunscreens," Australian Government, Therapeutic Goods Administration, TGA Fact Sheet: Sunscreens, August 2009.

5. *Materials and Sunscreens, Top Reasons for Precaution*, Friends of the Earth, August 19, 2009.

6. Waldman, Michael, Ph.D., Sean Nicholson, Ph.D., Nodir Adilov, Ph.D., and John Williams, M.D., M.B.A., "Autism Prevalence and Precipitation Rates in California, Oregon, and Washington Counties," *Arch Pediatr Adolesc Med.*, 2008, Vol. 162, Issue 11, 1026–1034.

11

Milk: Not for Human Consumption

"There's no reason to drink cows' milk at any time in your life. It was designed for calves, not humans, and we should all stop drinking it today."
—DR. FRANK A. OSKI (1932–1996),
Former Director of Pediatrics,
Johns Hopkins University

THE AMERICAN DAIRY ASSOCIATION has succeeded in getting consumers to believe that the healthy growth of their children depends on receiving calcium from cow's milk, and the dairy industry spends hundreds of millions of dollars every year to convince people to drink gallons of it. However, scientific evidence contradicts claims that milk products fulfill a nutritional requirement. Additionally, dairy products have major health drawbacks.

Milk:

- is frequently contaminated with antibiotics, growth hormones, drugs, pesticides, and dioxins.

- is directly linked to obesity, diabetes, heart disease, and certain cancers, including prostate cancer and breast cancer.
- may even cause osteoporosis—the very disease that the dairy industry says cow's milk helps to prevent—because the excess animal protein in dairy products leaches calcium from the bones.

The milk of cows is unique and specifically tailored to the requirements of baby cows (calves stop drinking milk between the ages of six to eight months). How species-specific is cow's milk? It has three to four times more protein than mother's milk, to allow for calves' rapid muscle growth. Yet cow's milk has only about one tenth the amount of essential fatty acids found in human milk, acids that are required for the development of your baby's brain and nervous system.

Anemia

Cow's milk products are very low in iron, and despite the American Academy of Pediatrics' misplaced enthusiasm for dairy products, even they recommend that infants under 1 year of age not receive whole cow's milk, as its consumption could lead an infant to develop iron deficiency anemia: to get the U.S. RDA of fifteen milligrams of iron, an infant would have to drink more than thirty-one quarts of milk per day, so in actuality, every milk serving is robbing your child of a chance to obtain iron from some other nutritional source.

Lactose Intolerance

By their fourth or fifth birthdays, many children lose the ability to digest the milk sugar lactose and develop uncomfortable gastrointestinal symptoms such as stomach pain, gas, bloating, and diarrhea after drinking and eating milk and dairy products. This set of symptoms is typically diagnosed as *lactose intolerance* and it's one of the most common causes of abdominal pain in children. Humans were never meant to drink milk after childhood and therefore the enzyme needed to digest the sugar in milk, from an evolutionary standpoint, is unnecessary after the first years, once children are weaned.

Note that not a single species in nature drinks milk beyond the age of weaning.

While doctors typically label all problems from milk consumption as lactose intolerance, many children may in actuality have milk protein allergies, in which case all milk and all other dairy products should be avoided.

Allergies

Food allergies appear to be a common result of milk consumption, particularly in children. The proteins in cow's milk are what provoke the allergies. As noted, cow's milk is meant for baby cows, whose intestines are naturally equipped to handle the milk's high protein levels. Human intestines are not intended to handle such proteins; in fact, these proteins may cause irritation and damage to the human intestinal lining. This in turn permits these proteins to be absorbed into the circulatory system. The immune system recognizes these proteins as foreign and attacks them, causing such symptoms as diarrhea, wheezing, or nasal congestion. A chronic runny nose from such congestion can then lead to the recurrent ear infections that plague so many children who are given cow's milk.

These allergic reactions to the proteins might even include minute gastrointestinal bleeding (sometimes so slight that it is missed). Over time, this bleeding reduces the body's iron stores and can be another cause of anemia in infants and young children.

Colic

Colic is much more common in babies receiving cow's milk-based formulas. As well, pediatricians learned long ago that breast-feeding mothers can have colicky babies if the mothers are drinking cow's milk. Research has shown that in situations where allergy-causing proteins in cow's milk pass through a mother's bloodstream into her breast milk and to the baby, some babies can react with colicky symptoms. Cow's milk should be suspected as a possible cause of fussy behavior in an otherwise normal, breast-fed baby.

Diabetes and Other Autoimmune Diseases

Some of the proteins in cow's milk share a resemblance to a human protein, which can turn the milk protein into "triggers" for auto-immune diseases, the result of which is that the human body literally attacks itself. Several reports link insulin-dependent diabetes to a specific protein in dairy products. A long-standing theory is that cow's milk proteins stimulate production of antibodies that, over time, cause an auto-immune reaction and destroy the insulin-producing cells of the pancreas.

Epidemiological studies of various countries show a strong correlation between the use of dairy products and the incidence of childhood diabetes. Another example of an autoimmune disease related to the ingestion of cow's milk is multiple sclerosis, where the body's response to bovine whey proteins is to destroy the myelin sheath, or outer membrane protecting nerve cells.

Saturated Fat

Most milk and dairy products contain significant amounts of saturated fat, contributing to cardiovascular diseases and certain forms of cancer. The early atherosclerotic changes of heart disease have been documented in American teenagers, who for the most part have been raised on a dairy-rich diet.

Contaminants

Milk contains frequent contaminants, including pesticides, antibiotics, and hormones. All mothers naturally pass hormones into their milk. While human hormones are meant for human infants, cow hormones are not. Equally problematic, synthetic hormones, such as recombinant bovine growth hormone, are commonly used in dairy cows to increase the production of milk. When the cows produce quantities of milk that nature never intended, they develop mastitis, or infection of the mammary glands. The cows are then given antibiotics. Hormones and antibiotics are therefore present in cow's milk and other dairy products, as are pesticides and other drugs.

Bone Health

New research casts grave doubt on the long-standing but poorly supported notion that dairy product consumption protects against bone loss. No consistent link has been found between the amount of calcium people consume and protection against osteoporosis.

Although dairy products are often cited by the dairy industry as being good sources of calcium to "help build strong bones," there is much debate over whether long-term consumption of dairy products helps bones at all. Dairy products offer a false sense of security to those concerned about calcium deficiency.

Several studies of teenagers have found that their bone health is related to their physical activity level earlier in life, but not to the amount of milk or calcium they consumed.

A 2000 study published in *Pediatrics* found that inactive teens had lower bone density by age 18 than those who engaged in regular physical activity. The researchers also found that the amount of calcium consumed (from milk or from other sources) had no effect on their bone density.[1]

> No consistent link has been found between the amount of calcium people consume and protection against osteoporosis.

A 2004 study published in the *Journal of Pediatrics* found that when eighty girls were followed for ten years starting at age 12, the only factor that influenced bone density was exercise. Calcium intake had no effect on bone strength.[2]

In countries where dairy products are not generally consumed (Asian countries such as China and Japan) there is actually less osteoporosis than in the United States. These are countries in which

iStock

Exercise is the most important factor in building bone strength.

people live as long as or longer than Americans and consume almost no calcium-rich dairy products. In Western countries that consume the most dairy foods—such as England and Finland—rates of osteoporotic fractures are among the highest in the world.[3] The Harvard Nurses Health Study looked at the milk-drinking habits of 72,000 women for twelve years, and found that regularly drinking milk did not translate to a lower risk of experiencing a hip fracture. In fact the women who consumed the most calcium from dairy foods broke more bones than those who rarely drank milk.

Milk does not build strong bones; in fact, the protein in the milk can actually damage bones. Too much animal protein actually causes a calcium drain, so high-protein dairy products can actually cause osteoporosis rather than preventing it. This is in keeping with the result of the Harvard Nurses Study and why people who consume dairy (and meat) have higher calcium requirements than vegetarians. Certainly, calcium intake is important, particularly during childhood, but the recipe for healthy bones clearly calls for more than simply ingesting copious amounts of milk and dairy. There are many non-dairy foods that are calcium-rich, such as broccoli and dark green leafy vegetables, nuts, beans, chickpeas, lentils, split peas, dried figs, and tofu.

Vitamin D

Although most people consider calcium to be the most important nutrient for strong bones, the fact is that good bone health is largely dependent on getting adequate vitamin D. Cow's milk in nature contains quite low levels, and almost all liquid milk sold commercially in the United States has chemically synthesized vitamin D_3 added. This is not true of other dairy products. As discussed in chapter dedicated to vitamin D and the benefits of sunshine, humans do not need to rely on milk or other parts of their diet for vitamin D, produced in the skin naturally after exposure to sunlight.

Gastroesophageal Reflux Disease (GERD)

Cow's milk consumption is a frequent cause of gastroesophageal reflux (GER), either from mothers passing cow proteins in their breast milk,[5] from milk formula feeding, or from liquid cow's milk given to toddlers. GER can cause colic and poor nutrient absorption. When more severe (known as GER disease or GERD), this dairy reaction can lead to feeding or sleeping problems, irritability, frequent crying as if in pain, arching of the back, frequent coughing and pneumonia, weight loss, or even failure to thrive.

For breast-fed babies who exhibit symptoms of reflux, cow's milk proteins must be eliminated from the mother's diet. As well, breast-feeding itself is a treatment for GERD, as breast milk empties quickly from the stomach and has characteristics that speed intestinal healing. Carrying an infant in a wrap or a sling to ensure a more upright posture is also a way to reduce reflux.

The American Academy of Pediatrics declares that the use of cow's milk before the first birthday causes a serious health risk to babies, that a substantial body of scientific evidence raises concerns about health risks from cow's milk products, and therefore babies under 1 year should never receive cow's milk.

According to the American Academy of Pediatrics, cow's milk:

- hinders the absorption of iron, causing iron-deficiency anemia

- is hard for human babies to digest.
- does not contain adequate nutrients for babies' health.
- contains protein that is allergenic to human babies.
- is deficient in vitamin E, crucial to healthy growth and development.
- is deficient in essential fatty acids (EFAs), crucial to healthy growth and development.
- contains protein levels that are too high for babies' growth and development.
- contains sodium levels that are too high for a baby's fragile system to handle. Too much sodium might cause an infant's kidneys to fail.
- contains protein that is very difficult for an infant to digest and absorb.
- can cause intestinal bleeding, leading to anemia from blood loss.

A reasonable person who considers all this evidence would find it difficult to believe that cow's milk is healthy for human babies on the day after their first birthday. However, despite *recognizing the many drawbacks* of cow's milk, the American Academy of Pediatrics recommends a diet laden with milk and dairy products after the first birthday. They recommend that four-year-olds should be drinking three eight-ounce glasses of milk per day,[6] and families should be consuming cheese or yogurt "for stronger bones and better bodies."[7]

The fact is, under scientific scrutiny, the myth of the healing powers of milk loses credibility. While milk is a fundamental, life-sustaining food for the young of every species of mammal, many people are now reconsidering using cow's milk and dairy as a form of human nourishment, realizing that there are alternatives that can replace these potentially harmful products.

Now you know . . .

There is no reason for your child to ever drink cow's milk. To build strong bones and healthy bodies, children need exercise, sunshine, and a diet rich in fruits and vegetables.

FOOTNOTES

1. Lloyd, T., V.M. Chinchilli, N. Johnson-Rollings, et al., "Adult female hip bone density reflects teenage sports-exercise patterns but not teenage calcium intake," *Pediatrics*, 2000, Vol. 106, Issue 40, 4.
2. Lloyd, T., et al., "Lifestyle factors and the development of bone mass and bone strength in young women," *Journal of Pediatrics*, June 2004, Vol. 144, Issue 6, 776–782.
3. Feskanich, D., W.C. Willett, M.J. Stampfe, G.A. Colditz, "Milk, dietary calcium, and bone fractures in women: a 12-year prospective study," *Am J Publ Health*, 1997, Vol. 87, 992–997.
4. Lanou, A.J., "Bone health in children," *BMJ*, October 14, 2006, Vol. 333, 763–764.
5. "Gastroesophageal Reflux and Cow Milk Allergy: Is There a Link?" *Pediatrics*, November 2002, Vol. 110, Issue 5, 972–984.
6. Greer, Frank R., M.D. and Nancy F. Krebs, M.D., "Optimizing Bone Health and Calcium Intakes of Infants, Children, and Adolescents," Committee on Nutrition, February 2006, *Pediatrics*, Vol. 117, Issue 2, 578–585 (doi:10.1542/peds.2005-2822).
7. The AAP endorses the *3-A-Day Campaign* from the National Dairy Council.

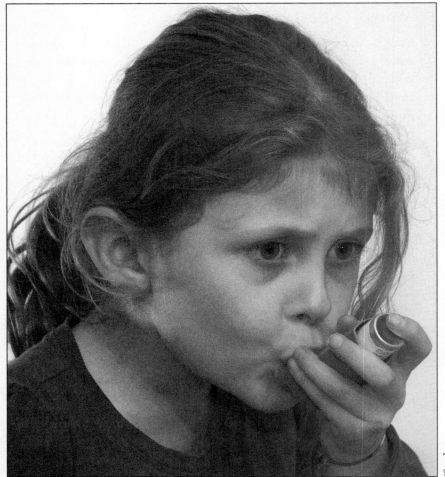

12

Allergies and Asthma

THE OCCURRENCE OF ALLERGIC DISEASES has increased dramatically over the past few decades, especially in children. This may be due in part to a rising consumption of processed and convenience foods, as well as in increase in pollutants (dust, chemicals from cleaners, and other possible allergens) in our contemporary environments.

What Are Allergies?

Allergies are an incorrect response on the part of your immune system, which recognizes substances such as pollen as foreign invaders to the body. When it comes in contact with these substances that would be otherwise harmless, the immune system has an unexpected hypersensitive reaction. There are hundreds of substances, or allergens, known to trigger allergies. These elements can affect the skin, eyes, respiratory system, and other organs.

One child in three is allergic today and hereditary factors play a big part in determining whether a child has allergies. However, the evolution of these diseases has been far too rapid for genetics to be the sole explanation, and children who have no known family history can still develop allergies. It is generally agreed that a combination of hereditary as well as *environmental* factors is responsible for the development of allergies.

Infants might show such allergy symptoms as nose rubbing, sniffles, sneezing, or congestion. As a result of allergies, a child might have recurrent sore throats and chronic ear infections. Food allergies can at other times cause rashes or intestinal problems.

Airborne Allergies

Allergic rhinitis, commonly known as *hay fever*, is the most common chronic childhood disease. Allergic illnesses are usually not life threatening, but they do put a strain on public health resources, work and school productivity, and the quality of life of the individuals concerned.

Two signs of allergic rhinitis in children are "allergic shiners" (dark circles under the eyes caused by increased blood flow near the sinuses) and the "allergic salute" (an upward movement of the hand against the nose that over time causes a crease mark on the nose). These are often accompanied by runny nose, cough due to post-nasal drip, watery eyes, and itchy eyes, nose, and throat.

Food Allergies

The Centers for Disease Control and Prevention (CDC) National Center for Health Statistics released a government report[1] in October 2008, stating that the number of children in the United States with food or digestive allergies had increased by 18 percent over the previous ten years.

As is the case with allergies in general, nobody knows why food allergies are becoming more and more common. Significant changes in Western diets during this period are considered to be a possible explanation. This may be related both to the way in which children are fed early in life as well as because more people are eating processed foods containing preservatives and additives.

The best thing that you can do for your children is to provide them with the foundation to live a healthy lifestyle. Eating the right foods can be a great start. Serve foods that are natural and from the earth rather than filled with additives and preservatives.

True food allergies, or those defined by one certain kind of antibody reaction (IgE), affect about 2 percent of children, although they are more common in younger children, affecting about 5 percent to 8 percent of them. The percentage of children who experience other kinds of food sensitivities or intolerance is far higher although it helps to bear in mind that many children will outgrow their food allergies by the time they are 3 years old.

While no one knows exactly why food allergies appear in some people and not others, one common factor is heredity. Generally, people with a food allergy come from families in which allergies are common—not necessarily food allergies, but perhaps hay fever, asthma, or hives. *If both parents have allergies, a child has about a 75 percent chance of being allergic as well*, according to the American College of Allergy, Asthma & Immunology. Meanwhile, if one parent or one side of the child's family has allergies, the risk drops to about 30 percent to 40 percent. Those with no family history of allergies run about a 10 percent to 15 percent risk of being allergic.

When trying to determine the food to which a child is allergic, parents often incorrectly assume that if the child has eaten a food before and has not had problems, then he's probably not allergic. Parents usually suspect only new foods as the cause of a food allergy. However, *a child must be exposed to a substance more than once to become allergic to it*. It takes time for the immune system to build up the "incorrect" response to something to which the body is eventually allergic. It may take days, weeks, months, or even years to build up enough of a response to cause noticeable symptoms. The offending food might be something that your child has eaten many times before without any reaction.

Food allergies in infants can cause such problems as crying, colic, vomiting, diarrhea, rashes, eczema, and congestion. Children with a food allergy are four times more likely to develop asthma or other types of allergies. Food allergic reactions sometimes simply cause mild gastrointestinal upset, but other reactions can range from a tingling sensation in the mouth to swelling of the lips and tongue, to hives, to difficulty breathing. The most serious reactions can progress to a drop in blood pressure, loss of consciousness, and even life-threatening complete systemic failure (anaphylaxis) in the most severe cases.

The single most common allergy among infants and children in the first year is to cow's milk proteins. Ninety-five percent of children's food allergies are due to eight foods:

- cow's milk
- egg whites
- wheat
- shellfish
- fish
- soy
- peanuts (not technically nuts but legumes in the same family as peas and beans)
- tree nuts (like almonds, walnuts, pecans, cashews).

Other common allergens include corn, citrus fruits, chocolate, and food additives.

Cut Out Dairy

As discussed in the previous chapter, cow's milk is an unhealthy food that is unnatural for the human body. Everyone is intolerant to it at some level. It is the leading cause of food allergy in the American diet. Many children with allergic rhinitis are actually suffering from cow's milk allergy. In fact, milk allergy appears to be responsible for a multitude of immune disorders, including asthma and eczema (eczema is discussed in the next chapter).

A milk allergy means your child's immune system is not tolerant of certain proteins found in milk products. There is no treatment for food allergy other than avoiding the food(s) in question. If you suspect that your child has a milk allergy, you need to completely eliminate milk, dairy products, and any foods with milk-containing ingredients from his diet, but this isn't always as simple as it sounds.

iStock

Nobody knows why food allergies are becoming more and more common.

It's important to check labels carefully for the following ingredients: milk, of course, as well as whey, dried milk solids, casein, lactalbumin, sodium caseinate, potassium caseinate, calcium caseinate, butter, cheese, margarine, and curds. In general, avoid any foods prepared with milk, cheese, butter, or cream.

What do you do if your child already has a food allergy?

- Once you know that there is a food allergy, strictly avoid that food, including any related products.
- Diligently read food labels (hidden ingredients, particularly with wheat and peanuts, can be anywhere, but the Food and Drug Administration requires that at least the top eight allergens must be clearly stated on food labels).
- Let servers in restaurants know that your child absolutely cannot have certain ingredients.

- If your child has severe food allergies, make sure they always carry or have readily available to them an epinephrine injector (often called an EpiPen Auto-Injector or simply EpiPen) in case of emergency.

During an episode of anaphylactic shock there is sudden severe swelling of the child's eyes, lips, and face that begins within a few seconds of exposure. Also, the throat may swell, making it difficult to breathe. *You must make sure your child has an EpiPen readily available if he suffers from severe allergic reactions to certain foods.* This can save his life if you are not within minutes of an emergency room. Peanuts, tree nuts, eggs, and shellfish are the main culprits in food-related anaphylactic shock in children. The main culprits of non-food ana-phylactic shock are bee and wasp stings, penicillin, and aspirin.

Preventing Food Allergies

Knowing that allergies and asthma tend to run in families, there are steps that families with a history of allergic disease can take to delay or reduce the occurrence of allergies in their infants.

We have already seen that exclusive breast-feeding—providing the infant with no other liquid or food other than breast milk—during the first six months brings many kinds of important protection to infants. Exclusive breast-feeding proves especially valuable for pre-venting allergies in children at high risk for being allergic—notably if one or both parents are affected by allergic disease.

The cow's milk proteins used in most artificial infant formulas are foreign to humans. When babies are exposed to non-human milk, these proteins pass through the baby's immature gastrointestinal tract and may be the predisposing factor in such illnesses as eczema and asthma. Multiple studies have suggested that babies who are breast-fed past six months of age have a lower probability of developing respiratory allergies, and this protection lasts into adolescence.

Soy formulas also commonly lead to allergic reactions, whether they are used as a first formula or in response to a milk formula aller-gy. Even formulas that have been hydrolyzed (meaning the proteins have been chemically broken down in the factory) can cause problems in highly sensitive babies. Avoiding artificial formulas of all kinds provides the best opportunity for avoiding allergies and reducing future asthma.

One study[2] suggests that exclusive breast-feeding for four months helps protect the child from cow's milk protein allergy until 18 months, reduces the likelihood of atopic dermatitis (skin allergy) until 3 years, and reduces the risk of recurrent wheeze (or asthma) until 6 years of age. However, the long-term effects of breast-feeding on allergic outcomes are not known and require investigation.

Identifying the Allergy

If you suspect that your child suffers from food allergies, but you can't identify the offending food, keep a record of what is being eaten, its ingredients if relevant, as well as subsequent related symptoms.

At present there are no medical tests for food allergies that are more accurate than dietary elimination and challenge. Elimination involves removing specific foods or ingredients from your child's diet that you suspect may be causing allergy symptoms. If you remove a certain food and the child's symptoms go away while following this diet, you can usually identify that food as the cause of your problems.

After following the elimination diet, you gradually reintroduce the foods you were avoiding into your child's diet, one at a time. This process helps link allergy symptoms to specific foods.

In most cases, carefully eliminating suspected culprits from your child's diet will uncover the food allergens. Many parents sometimes notice a paradox, and you may as well, that your child craves the very food to which he's allergic. In such cases, that food often constitutes a significant portion of the diet. As a result, the child will object strenuously to having that food removed, but after a period of adjustment, his resulting better sense of well-being ought to lead to acceptance. Often there is a threshold amount beyond which the child cannot eat the allergy-causing food, but infrequent or small portions do not cause problems.

A New Theory

In 2000, the American Academy of Pediatrics (AAP) feeding guidelines recommended that breast-feeding mothers of infants who are at high risk for developing allergies should avoid cow's milk, egg, fish, peanuts, and tree nuts from their own diets. Parents were also instructed that dairy products for children should be deferred until 1 year, eggs until 2 years, and peanuts, nuts, and fish until 3 years of age.

It was assumed that because a young child's digestive system had not yet matured, giving these foods to a child increased his body's likelihood of absorbing food proteins that might trigger allergies. Several new studies are challenging this theory: recent research suggests that early exposure to allergens actually prevents, rather than causes, food allergies.

A study of peanut allergy was the first one that suggested that introducing highly allergenic proteins early in life could create a tolerance to those particular antigens.

This large-scale 2008 study[3] was conducted in England, Israel, and the United States. It showed that *children who avoided peanuts in early childhood were ten times more likely to develop a peanut allergy than those who were exposed early and frequently to peanuts.* In other words, it now appears probable that children who consume peanuts early in infancy are *less* likely to develop a peanut allergy.

> *Recent research suggests that early exposure to allergens actually prevents, rather than causes, food allergies.*

The authors of this study point out that efforts at eliminating food allergens during pregnancy, lactation, and infancy have consistently failed to prevent food allergy and they hypothesize that early exposure might indeed be required to induce tolerance:

Paradoxically, past recommendations in the United States and current recommendations in the UK and Australia might be promoting the development of peanut allergy and could explain the continued increase in the prevalence of peanut allergy observed in these countries.

Our findings raise the question of whether early and frequent ingestion of high-dose peanut protein during infancy might prevent the development of peanut allergy through tolerance induction. In parts of the world where large quantities of peanuts are eaten, such as the Middle East, southeast Asia, and Africa, peanut allergy is rare.

Similarly, a trial of giving peanuts in order to overcome peanut allergy in children who are severely allergic has met with success in a British study.[4] The children were given small but gradually increasing doses of peanut flour to eat daily. After six months, each child was able to tolerate the ingestion of ten whole peanuts. The goal was not to enable the children to eat peanuts in great quantities at will, but rather to get them to the point where they would not be at risk for a severe reaction (anaphylaxis) if they accidentally ingested peanuts, such as at a restaurant or a birthday party.

The current research was undertaken by a team with a warning that the results are preliminary and the treatment should not be attempted outside research settings. The children were carefully monitored and epinephrine was available at all times in case of emergency.

Yet another study in 2009[5] showed that there was no association between early exposure to solid foods in the infant's diet and the development of eczema (a skin condition related to allergy) up to 4 years of age. This will be discussed further in the corresponding chapter.

Based upon these and other studies, in a move that surprised families of food-allergic children, the AAP in 2008 released new feeding guidelines that reversed prior recommendations.

After finding that delaying the introduction of solid foods, as previously recommended, did *not* lead to fewer food allergies among children at risk for developing allergies based on family history, the AAP released new guidelines that included the following:

- There is NO evidence for the use of soy for the prevention of allergy.
- While there is no change in the recommendation that solid foods should not be introduced before four to six months, delaying

the introduction of solids past six months shows no evidence of a protective benefit . . . this includes solids that are thought to be highly allergenic.

- After four to six months of age, there is not enough data to support dietary intervention (restriction).

Environmental Allergies

Because of limited exposure to the environment, there are few things to which infants may be allergic. The first environmental allergens that may affect children are indoor allergens. For instance, a major cause of allergy in infants and children is house dust mites—microscopic creatures that are found in large quantities inside the home. Other indoor allergens include pets and molds.

Once a child gets older, exposure to outside allergens, such as tree pollen, weeds, or grasses increases his chances of developing seasonal allergies because he spends more time outdoors.

For common environmental allergies, an allergy and asthma health specialist might know how best to analyze the symptoms and determine what types of environmental elements may be the suspected irritants.

"Allergic shiners" are a sign of allergies in children.

Preventing Environmental Allergies

Although many drugs are effective in treating allergies once they occur, many parents prefer not to rely solely on drug treatments for allergies and prefer a more preventive approach.

The World Health Organization (WHO) advises that preventive measures may go a long way in limiting the prevalence of environmental allergies. This includes avoiding exposure to tobacco smoke, especially during pregnancy and early childhood, as well as avoiding damp housing conditions, reducing indoor air pollutants, and generally eliminating irritating substances in the environment.

Try not to pollute your home and workplace with known allergens, especially if you suspect they are irritants. Carpets, upholstered furniture, and heavy drapes are major "reservoirs" for dust mites, pet fur, and tobacco residue that can trigger allergies.

House Dust

House dust aggravates allergies. It also contains many hazardous chemicals, including lead, fire retardants, pesticides, and other chemicals. Replacing wall-to-wall carpeting with materials that can be wiped clean (wood, tile, or non-vinyl linoleum) is helpful. If it is not feasible to remove carpeting, vacuum frequently, using a high-quality vacuum that has strong suction and a HEPA filter or at least a double-lined paper filter bag. Without a filter, the chemicals and pollutants just get re-circulated into the air.

Modifications at Home

You can take steps to reduce the occurrence of environmental allergens in your home by making such modifications as using zippered, plastic covers on pillows and mattresses and washing your bedding weekly in hot water. Indoor relative humidity should be kept low to inhibit dust mite population growth. Optimally, carpets, upholstered furniture, or objects that collect dust should be removed from your child's bedroom.

ALLERGY-FIGHTING FOODS

Foods high in *antioxidants* protect against allergies because the antioxidants scavenge potentially harmful molecules called free radicals from your body. Free radicals can cause oxidative tissue damage, which triggers inflammation and problems like allergies and asthma.

- Vitamin C acts as an antioxidant. Various fruits and vegetables such as oranges, apples, strawberries, grapefruit, cantaloupe, fresh tomatoes, broccoli, and Brussels sprouts are good sources of vitamin C.
- Vitamin E also acts as an antioxidant. Tree nuts are a particularly good source.
- Resveratrol is a powerful antioxidant found in peanuts and the skin of grapes.

The omega-3 fatty acids DHA and EPA, found in cold-water fish and algae sources, are anti-inflammatories. Wild salmon, mackerel, trout, herring, sardines, and albacore tuna are good sources of marine omega-3 fatty acids. As noted in Chapter 5, be mindful of concerns about mercury contamination when consuming fish.

Foods to Avoid

Avoid foods with partially hydrogenated oils (trans fats); these cause inflammation, making allergy symptoms worse.

Development of allergies to animals is associated with the presence of furry animals in the children's homes at birth. Animal allergies are triggered by proteins found in the secretions and dander (dried skin flakes) of certain animals with hair, including dogs, cats, and rabbits. As such, in an attempt to prevent allergies, infants at high risk because of family history should not be exposed to these indoor pets.

Asthma

In asthma, constriction of the muscles that line the air passages can lead to narrowed airways, in turn causing difficulty in breathing. In severe cases this can result in life-threatening reactions if the symptoms are not properly addressed through careful diagnosis and proper treatment. Although asthma and allergies can exist independently, asthma is a condition that is strongly linked to allergic reactions to such substances as dust, mold, animal dander, feathers, cigarette smoke, seasonal pollens and plants, aerosol sprays, and dairy products as well as other foods.

Yet asthma is a much more complex disease than simple allergies. Many other factors can trigger asthma attacks such as indoor or outdoor air pollution, exercise, sudden temperature changes, excitement, or stress. One is more likely prone to react to these asthma-triggering factors when already partly sensitized by allergens.

Asthma Prevention

Because allergies may trigger asthma, many of the steps taken to control allergies will also lessen the occurrence or severity of asthma in children.

Breast-feeding protects against asthma. Australian researchers completed a study in 2004[6] in which more than two thousand children were followed from birth through age 6. The key finding was that even after taking into account exposure to tobacco smoke, prematurity, gender, and family history, breast-feeding offers significant protection against asthma. Specifically, every additional month of exclusive breast-feeding (no formula) resulted in an additional 4 percent decrease in the chance of developing asthma.

Another study[7] on the Isle of Wight in the United Kingdom found that breast-feeding for at least four months helps protect children from asthma. Respiratory health was tracked in 15,000 British children born between 1989 and 1990, at the ages of 1, 2, 4, and 10. Those children who had been breast-fed for at least four months had significantly better lung function at the age of 10. The authors say that certain breast milk chemicals, which boost the developing child's immune system, may help explain the findings. They also point to the difference in impact on the lungs of suckling on a breast compared with sucking from a bottle. The duration of exercise a baby gets breast-feeding is almost twice as long as that for a bottle-fed baby. In addition to requiring less lung power, bottle feeding also induces a higher rate of swallowing and more interrupted breathing.

Maternal smoking during pregnancy and exposure to second-hand smoke in infancy has been shown to increase the incidence of wheezing as well as chronic respiratory illness in children, which includes ear infections.

It is beyond the scope of this book to discuss in detail the medical treatment of allergies and asthma. Prevention methods described above are always the first line of defense for these conditions. However, if symptoms are interfering with your child's lifestyle (school, sports, play) then seek proper medical advice from your pediatrician or allergy-and-asthma specialist. With appropriate education, prevention, and treatment, allergy and asthma symptoms can be well controlled.

Now you know . . .

Controlling allergies goes well beyond relying on drugs. Paying proper attention to diet and environmental conditions, taking steps to strengthen your child's immune system and avoiding things that weaken it, breast-feeding your baby, and avoiding cow's milk will go a long way toward preventing allergies in your child.

FOOTNOTES

1. Branum, Amy M., M.S.P.H. and Susan L. Lukacs, D.O., M.S.P.H., Centers for Disease Control and Prevention, NCHS Data Brief Number 10, October 2008, "Food Allergy Among U.S. Children: Trends in Prevalence and Hospitalizations."

2. "Nutrition and allergic disease," *Clinical and Experimental Allergy Reviews*, Vol. 6, 117–188, 2006 Blackwell Publishing Ltd.

3. Du Toit, "Early consumption of peanuts in infancy is associated with a low prevalence of peanut allergy," *J Allergy Clin Immunol.*, November 2008, Vol. 122, Issue 5, 984–991.

4. Lark, A.T., S. Islam, Y. King, J. Deighton et al., "Successful oral tolerance induction in severe peanut allergy," *Allergy*, August 2009, Vol. 64, Issue 8, 1218–1220.

5. Sariachvili, "Early exposure to solid foods and the development of eczema in children up to 4 years of age," *Pediatric Allergy and Immunology*, Vol. 21, Issue 1, Part I, 74–81.

6. Oddy, "The Relation of Breast-feeding and Body Mass Index to Asthma and Atopy in Children: A Prospective Cohort Study to Age 6 Years, American Journal of Public Health," September 2004, Vol. 94, No. 9, 1531–1537.

7. Ogbuanu, "Effect of breast-feeding duration on lung function at age 10 years: a prospective birth cohort study," *Thorax*, 2009, Vol. 64, 62–66.

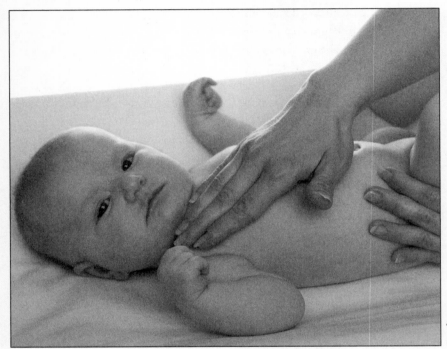

13

Atopic Dermatitis (Eczema)

ATOPIC (ALLERGIC) DERMATITIS, or eczema, is a distressing condition that usually starts during the baby's first year and affects about 10 percent of infants. The skin gets irritated, inflamed, itchy, red, and dry. Repeated scratching can tear the skin, leaving it susceptible to infection. And if the skin becomes infected it may crack and weep (leak fluid).

Atopic dermatitis most frequently appears when the child is between two and six months old. A baby with infant atopic dermatitis typically develops an itchy red rash on his face and scalp. This spreads over his face and down his neck, chest, and abdomen. When the child is 1½ to 2 years old, the disease will follow a more typical pattern, with the rash appearing behind his knees and in the bends of his arms, wrists, ankles, and neck. Extra folds are often observed just below the lower lid of both eyes. Called "atopic pleats" (also referred to as Dennie's lines or Dennie-Morgan folds), they are likely due to the rubbing and roughening that occurs with dry, itchy eyes.

Atopic dermatitis often occurs in phases. Most sufferers have periods of normal skin and then something will trigger the skin to flare up again.

Genetic Tendencies

The tendency to develop atopic dermatitis is inherited. While there is still some debate about what exactly causes atopic dermatitis, the most contemporary theory is that genetic factors lead to a defective skin barrier, leading to water loss and the subsequent typical symptoms of dryness and itchiness. Atopic dermatitis is quite common in babies, possibly because their skin is initially much thinner than that of adults.

The skin barrier keeps chemicals that come in contact with the skin from being absorbed into the body and it keeps water inside the skin from leaking out.

There appears to be a linked hereditary predisposition toward allergies, asthma, and atopic dermatitis. Children who get atopic dermatitis often have family members with allergic rhinitis (hay fever), asthma, or other allergies. Also, while most children eventually outgrow their atopic dermatitis, about half go on to develop one of these other conditions, which appear to be part of a series of immune disorders called the "atopic march." Over a period of years, a person may develop one and then another.

When children are already genetically predisposed to getting these conditions, environmental factors can certainly increase their risk. Typical triggers of atopic dermatitis are pollen, mold, excessive heat, rough fabrics, and possibly some foods (such as cow's milk, soy, eggs, fish, or wheat) yet this alone does not explain why there has been a tremendous increase in atopic dermatitis, as well as allergies and asthma, over the past decades. While researchers are not able to pinpoint the exact environmental or genetic risk factors that could be causing the increases, it could have something to do with the modern environment and pollution levels.

Treatments

Bathing—As distressing as it is to see your baby suffering with atopic dermatitis, the treatment can actually be quite simple. Atopic dermatitis steals moisture from the skin, so keep your child's skin moisturized as much as possible.

Using non-soap cleansers or a mild form of moisturizing soap is very useful in keeping your baby's skin moist. Choose cleansers and moisturizers that are fragrance-free and hypoallergenic, avoiding any that contain perfumes or dyes. After taking your baby out of the bath, his skin should not be completely dried. Lightly patting his skin with a towel to remove excess moisture is sufficient and preferable. Within three minutes of removing your child from the bath you should apply an emollient ("soothing" or "healing") lotion to his skin. This post-bath lotion application will allow moisture to penetrate his skin better and will likewise create a barrier against moisture from the bathwater evaporating from his skin.

Coconut Oil—An inexpensive emollient that works well, if you don't mind the greasiness, is coconut oil. Unprocessed virgin coconut oil is most effective and can be applied directly to the affected area of skin. It is rich in natural vitamins and has been used to moisturize skin for centuries. It has antiseptic and anti-inflammatory properties.[1] The fact that coconut oil results in absolutely no side effects makes this an even more attractive option.

African Black Soap—With a rising interest in natural, biodegradable beauty products, African Black Soap, handmade for thousands of years in villages all over Africa, is growing in popularity with Western consumers. It is excellent for babies with atopic dermatitis.

The soap is made with virgin palm kernel oil, residues from making unrefined shea butter, cocoa pods, and plantain leaf ashes. Plantain, a popular food in Africa that looks much like a banana, is a rich source of vitamins A and E and iron.

The plantains are roasted in a kettle over an open fire, along with cocoa pods, and the soap retains the ashes from the burnt dried leaves and pods, which gives it deep black and brown variations in color. The longer the plantains are roasted, the darker the soap. While most authentic African Black Soaps are actually closer to brown in color, the name "black soap" has stuck. After being hand-stirred by local women for at least a day, the soap is then set out to cure for two weeks.

Be cautious of soaps that are labeled as black soap or African Black Soap but are manufactured in the United States, Europe, or Asia on a large scale. These soaps are not authentic African Black Soap. It is important to look at the list of ingredients and make sure they contain shea butter and palm or coconut oil rather than any cheap oils or fats. Also, determine how the black color was obtained. The dark color of a true, original black soap is obtained by the lengthy traditional method. It is not economical to use the traditional method in an industrial setting, so charcoal or black dyes are added to mimic the authentic dark color.

Bleach—Because of the defective skin barrier, the skin of children with atopic dermatitis is often colonized with Staphylococcus aureus bacteria. This is one of the factors contributing to the flares of this condition.

In a 2009 study,[2] a group of researchers found that children treated twice-weekly with baths in diluted bleach showed a reduction in atopic dermatitis. In fact, the results were so remarkable and so quick that the Northwestern University study was terminated early so that the placebo group could benefit. The children in the study, who were aged six months to 17 years, were bathed in a tub of either plain water (about forty gallons) or in water with about half a cup of bleach. Bleach that is not diluted can burn the skin, but at the level recommended it would be hard to even tell that it was in the water.

Among the children who had the bleach baths, the study found a reduction in atopic dermatitis severity that was five times greater than those in the placebo group—but only on the body, not the face, because they were not submerging their heads. Children who take the baths should close their eyes and mouths and put their heads in the water, too, the researchers said.

If your child is suffering from eczema, should you try a bleach bath?

Given that bleach's antibacterial properties can improve a child's skin infection from *Staph* bacteria, the diluted bleach bath makes sense. Studies have found a correlation between the number of bacteria on the skin and eczema's severity. However, bleach can be hazardous. When not sufficiently diluted, the fumes and the liquid can irritate the eyes, ears, nose, mouth, throat, airways, and lungs. Chlorinated household cleaners (such as bleach) can react with other cleaners and form compounds that are toxic and/or cancer causing.

Also, a bleach bath doesn't address the cause of eczema. So it may provide relief, but it won't solve the problem. It is just one of the several treatments that you can consider while also looking for food allergies and common triggers. Make sure to store any bleach products out of reach of children.

Caution with Baby Bath Products—Not All Are Gentle

Even common "safe, gentle, and mild" products such as shampoos and washes often contain harmful ingredients such as perfumes and preservatives that can cause skin reactions.

In a 2009 report,[3] the Campaign for Safe Cosmetics (CSC) describes lab tests that found that 61 percent of the children's shampoos, lotions, soaps and other personal care products tested contained the chemicals formaldehyde and 1,4-dioxane. The report said that "these chemicals, which can be absorbed through the skin, are widely recognized as carcinogens in animal studies, and

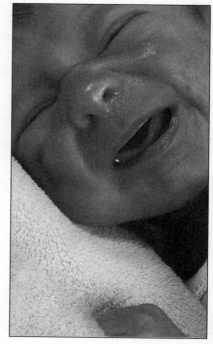

Atopic dermatitis most frequently appears when the child is between two and six months old.

iStock

expert panels consider them to be known or probable human carcinogens...Formaldehyde can also trigger skin reactions, such as
contact dermatitis...These two chemicals, linked to cancer and skin
allergies, are anything but safe and gentle and are completely un-
regulated in children's bath products."

The chemicals often don't appear on product labels. One reason
is that retail products aren't required to list individual ingredients of
"fragrances." Another reason is that some of the chemicals are by-
products of manufacturing and not considered ingredients, as such.

Vegetable Oil

As an emollient, you can add a few drops of plain vegetable oil (saf-
flower or coconut oil) into the bath water after the first few minutes.
(Be careful because bath oils result in slippery conditions.)

Oatmeal

An oatmeal bath is an effective remedy to relieve dryness. Tie up
a sock containing some oatmeal and put it in the bath water. As
the oatmeal colloid diffuses into the water, it is very soothing to the
baby's skin and will reduce any itching.

Clothing

After bathing, children should be dressed in soft clothes made of 100
percent cotton. Clothing your baby in cotton rather than in synthetic
or woolen materials will enable your baby's skin to breathe and help
to reduce irritation.

Burow's Solution

Burow's solution 1:40 is a commonly used antiseptic wet dressing
for the treatment of infected skin that leaks fluid, or weeps. It can be
bought over the counter in any pharmacy. The solution is prepared
easily by dissolving one Domeboro packet or effervescent tablet in a

pint of tepid or lukewarm tap water. Submerge a soft cloth (handkerchief, thin diaper, strips of bed sheets) into the solution until moderately wet but not dripping. Place the dressing over the affected skin site, periodically re-wetting the compress.

Environment

Environmental sensitivities and allergies are hard to avoid but important to identify. Some, such as secondhand smoke, animal dander, and household cleaners are easy to eliminate and control for most households. Dust control was discussed previously. Mold is harder to avoid, particularly because it is often hidden, but because it requires moisture to live and grow, reducing moisture in the home is the most effective way to combat mold.

A 2009 exploratory study[4] in the *British Journal of Dermatology* suggested that nylon clothing, dust, unfamiliar pets, sweating, and shampoos may play a direct role in worsening atopic dermatitis in children with the condition. Combinations of exposures acting in concert may also be important.

Proper Nutrition

Atopic dermatitis is sometimes related to food allergies. If a particular food is thought to cause atopic dermatitis, that food should be avoided. Breast milk is the best choice for infants, because babies are not allergic to their mother's milk (although they can be allergic to something that she is eating).

A clinical report from the American Academy of Pediatrics[5] recommended exclusive breast-feeding during the infant's first four months to prevent development of atopic dermatitis in infants at high risk of developing allergy.

As with allergies (discussed in the previous chapter), the foods most likely to cause atopic dermatitis are dairy, eggs, citrus, wheat, soy, chocolate, peanuts, and tree nuts. These foods are not essential to a healthy diet. Colorful fruits and vegetables, whole grains, and vegetable proteins will provide the nutrients needed for a child's cell growth and immune functioning.

Early Introduction of Solid Foods

In years past, mothers were told to delay introducing their child to solid foods until he was at least 1 or even 2 or 3 years old. However, there is currently *no* evidence that avoidance of certain foods will prevent the eventual development of allergic diseases, including eczema.[6] You should still breast-feed for as long as possible (exclusive breast-feeding without formula supplementation for at least four months), because breast-feeding helps the baby's immune system to develop properly. Yet it now appears that solid food may be introduced at six months of age without increasing the risk for eczema or the risk of becoming sensitized to foods later.

Essential Fatty Acids (EFAs)

Essential Fatty Acids are one type of the lipids (beneficial fats) that make up the skin barrier. EFAs are critical to maintaining healthy skin and combating inflammation. EFAs are involved in enzyme regulation, the absorption of nutrients in the cells, the creation of cell membranes, and cell communication.

The typical American diet contains relatively few sources of the important omega-3 EFAs. Breast-fed babies obtain their EFAs through breast milk. Older children can get their EFAs from foods such as cold water fish (herring, black cod, salmon, and sardines), and vegetarian sources such as nuts, seeds, and flax seed oil.

The omega-3 fatty acids EPA and DHA (found in fish oil) can decrease production of inflammation in our bodies. Any inflammatory condition—including atopic dermatitis—may improve with fish oil supplementation.

Recent research, including a 2008 study published in the *British Journal of Dermatology*,[6] showed that a diet rich in omega-3 can help atopic dermatitis sufferers reduce the severity of their symptoms. Patients given purified fish oil supplements had a statistically significant improvement in their symptoms.

Probiotics

Babies' guts are colonized by bacteria after birth, and acquiring the right balance of the different bacterial strains is important for developing an effective gut immune system.

Probiotics are microscopic living organisms—in most cases mixtures of "good" or "healthy" bacteria—that help maintain the natural balance of organisms (microflora) in the intestines. The World Health Organization defines probiotics as "live microorganisms, which, when administered in adequate amounts, confer a health benefit on the host."

The largest group of probiotic bacteria in the healthy intestine is lactic acid bacteria, of which *Lactobacillus acidophilus* is the best known.

While scientific understanding of probiotics and their potential for preventing and treating health conditions is still at an early stage, evidence does suggest that probiotics can help prevent atopic dermatitis. Clinical studies[7] have found that when babies who have a family history of allergic conditions are given probiotic bacteria, fewer of them go on to develop atopic dermatitis.

Breast milk contains natural probiotic substances, another reason that exclusively breast-fed babies are less likely to develop eczema. Mothers should consider breast-feeding for as long as possible if their child is susceptible to skin problems.

Probiotic Foods

Most probiotic food is fermented, at least partially. Among foods containing probiotics:

- **Tempeh** is a fermented soy product that has the chewy texture of meat. Unlike tofu, tempeh uses whole soybeans that are allowed to ferment (a type of beneficial mold forms that binds the soy together). Tempeh can be used in many vegetarian dishes as a high-quality protein and is one of the few vegetarian sources of vitamin B12.

- **Miso** is a Japanese seasoning that is produced by fermenting various beans or grains. It is used in soups, sauces, and spreads.
- **Sauerkraut** is fermented or pickled cabbage. Fresh cabbage is generally cut and then allowed to ferment in brine for a period of time.
- **Some fruit juices** are specifically manufactured with added probiotic cultures.

Zinc

Zinc is one of the most important nutrients for immune function and skin health. It is vital for wound healing, which is especially important when treating eczema. Dietary sources of zinc include nuts, seeds (such as pumpkin seeds), egg yolks, ginger, split peas, fruits, asparagus, and spinach.

Steroids

Corticosteroids are powerful drugs closely related to cortisol, a hormone that is naturally produced in the adrenal gland. Corticosteroids act on the immune system by blocking the production of substances that trigger allergic and inflammatory actions. Many doctors suggest topical use of corticosteroid (also called steroid) creams. These are intended to lessen inflammations in the skin and are used for an assortment of skin rashes, including atopic dermatitis.

Steroids offer temporary relief for a long-term problem. They are not a cure as they have no effect on the underlying cause of the inflammation. These powerful medications do not cure atopic dermatitis; they are only used to suppress the associated symptoms, such as redness and itchiness. Once the treatment is stopped, the atopic dermatitis is likely to come back after a few days.

Your children depend on you to keep them safe. Always read the precautions and full list of potential side effects before accepting a steroid cream as part of a course of treatment.

There are many possible side effects of using creams containing steroids:

- Steroids work by interfering with the body's inflammation response. However, they also impede the function of white blood cells that destroy foreign bodies and help keep the immune system functioning properly. The interference with white blood cell function yields a side effect of increased susceptibility to fungal or bacterial infections of the skin. Topical steroids should never be used to treat inflamed skin that is also infected.
- A thinning of the skin is the most typical side effect of steroid cream use. If this condition occurs, it usually reverses itself when the steroid is stopped. However, when used on a long-term basis, permanent stretch marks, bruises, skin discoloration, or spider veins may develop.

What we apply to the skin is also absorbed into the body, especially in babies. This is because baby skin is thinner and more porous than adult skin. A baby's skin surface area, which is large relative to his body weight, also means that steroids in creams applied all over his body can potentially reach high concentrations in his blood.

> What we apply to the skin is also absorbed into the body, especially in babies. This is because baby skin is thinner and more porous than adult skin. A baby's skin surface area, which is large relative to his body weight, also means that steroids in creams applied all over his body can potentially reach high concentrations in his blood.

Before using a steroid medicine, caregivers should work with a pediatrician to see if the baby's skin condition is caused by a nutritional deficiency, food allergy, or irritation from soaps or moisturizers.

When to Contact the Doctor

Make an appointment with your pediatrician or dermatologist if:

- atopic dermatitis does not respond to non-prescription treatments discussed in this chapter;
- symptoms worsen; or
- your child has signs of infection (such as blisters, oozing, redness, pain).

Outlook

Most children (up to 80 percent) will grow out of their atopic dermatitis before they reach adolescence, although they might experience itchy or inflamed skin if exposed to irritants as adults.

Now you know...

Relying on medical treatment alone for atopic dermatitis is only moderately effective and can involve significant side effects. Pharmaceuticals never cure this disease completely and just give short term relief. Attention to daily skin care, proper nutrition, and strengthening the immune system will go a long way toward reducing the occurrence and severity of atopic dermatitis.

FOOTNOTES

1. Marina, A.M., Y.B. Man, S.A. Nazimah, and I. Amin. "Antioxidant capacity and phenolic acids of virgin coconut oil," *Int J Food Sci Nutr.*, December 2008, 29:1–10.
2. Huang, et al., "Treatment of *Staphylococcus aureus* Colonization in Atopic Dermatitis Decreases Disease," *Pediatrics,* 2009, 123: 808–814.
3. Campaign for Safe Cosmetics report, "No More Toxic Tub," March 2009
4. Langan, S.M., P. Silcocks, and H.C. Williams, *British Journal of Dermatology*, Vol. 161, Issue 3, 640–646.

5. Greer, F.R., S.H. Sicherer, and A.W. Burks,"Effects of early nutritional interventions on the development of atopic disease in infants and children: the role of maternal dietary restriction, breast-feeding, timing of introduction of complementary foods, and hydrolyzed formulas," *Pediatrics*, January 2008, Vol. 121, Issue 1, 183–91.

6. Sariachvili, "Early exposure to solid foods and the development of eczema in children up to 4 years of age," *Pediatric Allergy and Immunology*, Vol. 21, Issue 1, Part I, 74–81.

7. Koch, C., S. Dölle, M. Metzger, C. Rasche, H. Jungclas, R. Rühl, H. Renz, M. Worm, "Docosahexaenoic acid (DHA) supplementation in atopic atopic dermatitis: a randomized, double-blind, controlled trial," *British Journal of Dermatology*, April 2008, Vol. 158, Issue 4, 786–792.

8. "Baby-friendly bacteria can help prevent development of eczema," Early Nutrition Programming Symposium, Granada, April 23, 2008.

14

Ear Infections

IN THE FIRST TWO YEARS the average child consumes an astounding three month's worth of antibiotics for otitis media, better known as ear infections. In the United States, the practice of prescribing antibiotics for ear infections has become almost universal in recent years, although it remains controversial in other nations. The frequent diagnosis and treatment of otitis media is having a huge effect on both our environment and the children treated who collectively receive more than thirty million courses of antibiotics for ear infections each year. More troubling is that the routine administration of antibiotics has caused a skyrocketing incidence of resistant bacteria (*superbugs*), which is making many of these medicines useless.

Wouldn't it be wonderful if there were a way to cut the incidence of antibiotic use for otitis media? In fact, there is.

Over-Diagnosis

The most effective solution for cutting antibiotic use for ear infection would be for pediatricians to be more accurate in their diagnoses. Much of the time, ear infections are diagnosed when they don't really exist.

Most of the unnecessary and inappropriate antibiotic use associated with treating "ear infections" comes from treating conditions that are thought to be acute otitis media but are actually some other illness, such as a viral upper respiratory tract infection, which cannot be treated with antibiotics and will go away on its own. If a crying child with a respiratory infection has a low-grade fever, his eardrum upon examination will almost invariably show some abnormality due to either the crying itself or some middle ear fluid, neither of which automatically points to an ear infection.

There are many inappropriate diagnoses and treatments of supposed ear infections. Here are a few facts to consider:

- Much of what qualifies as otitis media is in actuality part of the natural history of a cold and resolves quickly without any specific treatment.
- When an office or emergency room physician is faced with a fussy child and exhausted parents, it is common for that doctor to give a diagnosis of otitis media.
- The diagnosis of acute otitis media is not always certain, especially if the child is crying or has a fever, both of which can cause the eardrums to become red, mimicking a primary sign of ear infections.
- Pediatricians often give an antibiotic because they feel under pressure to do so, believing it is what the parent wants.
- It is easier and less time-consuming for a doctor to write a prescription than to explain why it is not necessary.

Symptoms

As problematic as incorrectly treating an ear infection during a *sick* visit, a pediatrician sometimes diagnoses one during a *well* visit for a child whose "eardrum looks a little bit pink" yet is otherwise exhibiting no other symptoms of otitis media.

The fact is, ear infections are almost always preceded by congestion due to a cold or allergy. It takes a few days for fluid to build up in the middle ear and then become infected, so it's likely premature to diagnose an ear infection within the first few days of those symptoms.

Another way to differentiate between discomfort from a cold or allergy and an ear infection is the pain: ear infections are painful. That pain stems from your baby lying flat, which prevents built-up fluid from draining from his middle ear. This in turn leads to a fussy and eventually difficult to console baby who, unlike an older child, cannot communicate the source of his discomfort.

If your child does not have an upper respiratory infection, ear pain, or fever, then it is unlikely that your child has an ear infection, or has a significant one. A baby "pulling at the ears" is *not* a sign of an ear infection. They often touch their ears out of habit or due to teething discomfort.

Causes

Otitis media is chiefly a disease of infancy, and children will usually have fewer problems with the infections after the age of 3. Ear infections are common in infants and children in part because their Eustachian tubes become clogged easily. For each ear, a Eustachian tube runs from the middle ear to the back of the throat. Its purpose is to drain fluid and bacteria that normally occur in the middle ear. If the Eustachian tube becomes blocked, fluid can build up and bacteria can take the opportunity to overgrow, causing infection. Anything that causes the Eustachian tubes and upper airways to become inflamed or irritated, or cause more fluid to be produced, can lead to a blocked Eustachian tube. Causes of the blockage might include colds (upper respiratory infections), allergies, tobacco smoke, the use of pacifiers, being formula- rather than breast-fed, feeding your baby while he's lying down, and, more broadly, exposing your child to sick children in daycare or other similar childcare situations. As children mature, their Eustachian tubes become more vertical; this allows for better drainage from the middle ear to the back of the throat, decreasing the likelihood of middle ear fluid accumulation.

Prevention

There are many things you can do to minimize the incidence of ear infections:

- **Breast-feed.** Breast milk contains antibodies that offer protection from ear infections. Exclusive breast-feeding until at least three months of age reduces the incidence of otitis media, and this effect persists four to twelve months after breast-feeding ceases.[1]
- **Avoid sick children.** Limiting daycare exposure for very young children decreases the risk of upper respiratory tract infection, which can in turn develop into otitis media. Children in large daycare programs tend to have more ear infections than children in smaller groups.[2]
- **Avoid secondhand smoke.** Children exposed to smoke have more episodes of otitis media than children not exposed. Secondary smoke in the home causes irritation of the respiratory tract, so make sure that no one smokes in your home. When away from home, stay in smoke-free environments.
- **Minimize incidence of environmental or food allergies.** Up to a third of all cases of ear infections are due to dairy or milk allergies. Other foods may be suspect, but the frequent connection between dairy and ear infections suggests that the elimination of dairy is a good first strategy. Other allergens in the environment, such as dust and feathers, can be eliminated by the methods listed in Chapter 12.
- **Get rid of the pacifier.** Children under 3 who use pacifiers run a 25 percent greater risk of getting ear infections. In a June 2008 published study,[3] researchers in The Netherlands found that recurrent ear infections occurred nearly twice as frequently in babies and young children who used pacifiers than in those who did not. Pacifier use contributes to otitis media by making it more likely for viruses and bacteria to be sucked into the middle ear. Avoid the use of a pacifier, prolonged sucking on a bottle, or even a "sippy-cup." Drinking while lying flat is unnatural and can cause fluid build-up in the middle ear.

EUROPE AND ANTIBIOTICS

After diagnosing an ear infection, pediatricians in Europe usually wait several days before considering an antibiotic prescription. The research has shown that when this technique is used, the infections take the same amount of time to get better as when giving antibiotics right away.

Antibiotics

Routine administration of antibiotics for the treatment of ear infections has recently come under scrutiny because, although otitis media is a common childhood complaint, most ear infections resolve themselves without the need for antibiotics.

A dramatic study negated the need for antibiotic treatment for ear infections. The landmark study,[4] published in *Pediatrics*, showed that treating non-severe ear infections (temperature is less

> Most ear infections resolve themselves without the need for antibiotics.

than 102.2 and pain is not severe) with antibiotics has no benefit when compared to doing nothing. In this study, 223 children were divided into two groups. One group received antibiotics; the other group received only medicines for symptom relief.

Results of the study were dramatic. No difference was observed between the two groups in days of work or school missed, visits to doctors' offices or emergency rooms, or number of phone calls to pediatricians. There was no difference in the recurrence rate by day thirty, and no difference in the clinical examination of the children's eardrums at day thirty.

This study clearly showed that antibiotics are not necessary or beneficial in the management of non-severe ear infections.

Wait-and-See Approach

In light of the fact that a large majority of children with acute otitis media recover without antibiotics, the American Academy of Pediatrics (AAP) and the American Academy of Family Physicians (AAFP) issued a joint statement in March 2004 on how to treat patients with ear infections. These organizations now recommend a *wait-and-see* approach for the first seventy-two hours after diagnosis. That suggestion holds for children who:

- are older than age six months. This age was chosen as the lower age limit because there's limited data on this approach in younger children and severe illness is more difficult to recognize;
- are otherwise healthy; and
- have mild signs and symptoms or an uncertain diagnosis.

The guidelines are based on several studies conducted over the course of many years, concluding that 80 percent to 90 percent of ear infections heal by themselves without antibiotics. The majority of episodes are caused by viruses as part of an upper respiratory viral infection, and so do not respond to antibiotics, which treat only bacterial infections. Also, *fluid persists in the middle ear for weeks or months after acute otitis media*, but this is expected and is not helped by the administration of more antibiotics.

The 2004 guidelines advise physicians in a majority of cases to send patients home with a recommendation for no more than a nonprescription pain reliever and directions to observe the patient.

Other parts of the guidelines suggest that pediatricians and family practice physicians should encourage families to reduce risk factors that might lead to ear infections. Breast-feeding for at least six months, avoiding "bottle propping," and eliminating exposure to passive tobacco smoke are all ways to reduce the risks for babies and infants.

Your pediatrician may recommend an antibiotic if your child is younger than six months, only because babies of that age have not been studied for the wait-and-see approach. You can discuss this with your doctor if such a situation arises.

Despite the official recommendations of the wait-and-see approach and the fact that it's based on years of scientific study, most pediatricians don't take this approach and continue to write millions of unnecessary prescriptions, according to a report[5] by the Agency for Healthcare Research and Quality, a U.S. government agency charged with "advancing excellence in healthcare." One study showed that only 6 percent of doctors used the wait-and-see approach frequently.[6]

> Despite the official recommendations of the wait-and-see approach and the fact that it's based on years of scientific study, most pediatricians don't take this approach and continue to write millions of unnecessary prescriptions, according to a report by the Agency for Healthcare Research and Quality, a U.S. government agency charged with "advancing excellence in healthcare."

The Problem with Antibiotics

In most cases antibiotics do more harm than good, leading to side effects, resistance to the drugs, and a cycle of hard-to-treat and recurring infections. As noted, antibiotics are only effective against bacterial infections, not viral ones. A large number of ear infections are caused by viruses. Further, when antibiotics kill bacteria, they are not selective. They don't always kill all the bad bacteria while they always kill plenty of good bacteria.

An ear infection caused by bacteria often contains some "resistant" bad bacteria that are not destroyed by the chosen antibiotic. These organisms can then thrive in the back of the nose and throat, so a child is more likely to develop a second infection within a month after treatment.

The antibiotic may also kill many of the beneficial microflora in the intestines, and when this good bacteria is eliminated, the child very often suffers from such gastrointestinal problems as diarrhea and yeast overgrowth.

Exposure to bacterial and viral infections allows your child's immune system to develop the antibodies needed to fight off future infections. Antibiotics may interfere with this process, leaving your child's body vulnerable later on. We are likely seeing an increase in ear infections because antibiotic use is on the rise.

Studies have shown that children whose ear infections are treated with antibiotics are more likely to have recurrences of the ear infections.[7]

Alternative Treatment

Because most ear infections do not need antibiotics, the goal of treatment is the alleviation of pain until the infection subsides.

If your child is uncomfortable, you can give him an over-the-counter pain reliever or obtain a prescription for pain-relieving eardrops that contain a local anesthetic that will temporarily numb the affected area. The drops won't cure the infection, but they will relieve pain and allow time for the infection to clear up naturally. If necessary, parents can use ear drops in conjunction with either ibuprofen (Motrin) or acetaminophen (Tylenol). Consult your pediatrician about these combinations and, during the wait-and-see period, also call your doctor if your child is still running a fever after forty-eight to seventy-two hours and is still in pain.

Australian researchers reported in 2008[8] that topical anesthetic (lidocaine HCl) ear drops give rapid relief of ear pain with peak effect within two to five minutes, and last for thirty to forty-five minutes. If using the drops, warm them up slightly by placing the drops bottle in warm water. Then gently lay your child on a flat surface with his infected ear facing up and administer the drops as directed.

Because heat alone is helpful in relieving pain, a few drops of gently-heated oil (baby oil, mineral oil, vegetable, garlic, or olive oil) in the ear canal will have a soothing effect on the inflamed tympanic membrane (eardrum).

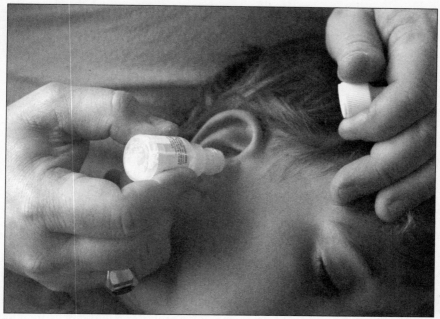

iStock

Ear infections are painful. Ear drops that contain a local anesthetic will temporarily numb the pain.

Tympanostomy Tubes

Often when a child experiences recurrent ear infections or chronic fluid in the ear, he will be referred to the otolaryngologist (ear, nose, and throat or ENT doctor) who will make arrangements to place tubes in your child's ear. Tympanostomy tube insertion is the most common procedure requiring general anesthesia for U.S. children, with more than half a million surgeries done each year. The surgery involves small implants—tympanostomy tubes—that are open at both ends. The tubes are inserted into eardrum incisions made by the surgeon. Tubes come in various shapes and sizes and are made of plastic or metal. They are left in place until they fall out by themselves or until they are removed by a doctor.

Medical experts are divided on the need for ear tube surgery. Official guidelines from the American Academy of Otolaryngology–Head and

Neck Surgery list presence of persistent middle ear fluid for more than three months as a reason to recommend surgery. Tubes are also suggested when there have been multiple episodes of acute otitis media (at least three episodes in six months or four episodes in twelve months).

Tube placement in children does not treat the underlying problem that led to the ear disease nor does it remedy the condition that led to the surgical intervention. Rather, the inserted tube keeps fresh air circulating in the middle ear until the child grows and the Eustachian tube function normalizes.

Overuse and Problems

In the past, doctors have been concerned that if surgery was not used in the case of persistent middle ear fluid, children could face long-term developmental impairment: parents were warned that if fluid in the middle ear lingered after treatment of an ear infection it could impair hearing and cause speech and language delay as well as problems with learning and behavior.

However, well-planned studies have challenged many of the assumptions that long justified the use of tympanostomy tubes. Ear disease does not cause developmental problems, and there are no studies that show that there is a true and lasting benefit to children who receive the tubes.

Placing ear tubes in young children who develop fluid in the ears does not improve speech, hearing, or psychological development, according to research. Dr. Jack L. Paradise, Professor Emeritus of Pediatrics at Children's Hospital of Pittsburgh, and other independent researchers have found no lasting effects of lingering fluid in the middle ear in otherwise healthy children.

"The decision to undergo ear tube surgery should be discussed carefully with the doctor," says Dr. Paradise. "A variety of factors go into this decision. If you think putting tubes in the child's ears is going to improve developmental outcome at age 3, the answer is: no, it won't."

"There is absolutely no evidence of long-term benefit with tube placement for otitis media," agrees Robert M. Jacobson, M.D., chair of the Department of Pediatrics at the Mayo Clinic in Rochester, Minnesota. "We need to avoid treatment of ear infections with tympanostomy tubes."

Lawrence Kleinman, M.D, M.PH., vice chair for research and education and associate professor of health policy and pediatrics at Mount Sinai School of Medicine in New York City, says, "In a study from 2002, in nine out of ten cases, tubes would not have been recommended, according to the American Academy of Pediatrics treatment guidelines."[9]

Ear tube surgery does have risks: the small but real risk of complications from the general anesthesia and concern about the long-term effect of the artificial implant in the eardrum. Minor degrees of eardrum scarring happen in almost one-third of children with tympanostomy tubes, though this usually does not result in any change in the way the eardrum functions. There is also concern about the persistent holes in the eardrum that can exist even after the tympanostomy ear tubes have come out on their own, sometimes requiring more surgery to repair the eardrum. If the past is any guide, children are likely to continue to get ear tubes they don't need.

Robert M. Jacobson, M.D., chair of the Department of Pediatrics at the Mayo Clinic in Rochester, Minnesota: "We need to avoid treatment of ear infections with tympanostomy tubes."

Now you know...

The best course is to find out the likely cause of your child's ear problem and to treat the underlying problem rather than relying on multiple courses of antibiotics or tympanostomy tubes. At the first sign of an ear infection, or if your child has had chronic problems in the past, it is worth considering risk factors that may be exacerbating those problems and eliminating as many of those factors as possible.

FOOTNOTES

1. Aniansson, G., B. Alm, B. Andersson, et al., "A prospective cohort study on breast-feeding and otitis media in Swedish infants," *Pediatr Infect Dis J*, 1994, Vol. 13, 183–188; Duncan, B., J. Ey, C.J. Holberg, A.L.Wright, F.D. Martinez, and L.M. Taussig,"Exclusive breast-feeding for at least four months protects against otitis media," *Pediatrics*, 1993, Vol. 91, 867–872; Duffy, L.C., H. Faden, R. Wasielewski, J. Wolf, D. Krystofik," Exclusive breast-feeding protects against bacterial colonization and day care exposure to otitis media," *Pediatrics*, 1997,Vol. 100, E7.

2. Owen, M.J., C.D. Baldwin, P.R. Swank, A.K Pannu, D.L. Johnson, V.M. Howie, "Relation of infant feeding practices, cigarette smoke exposure, and group child care to the onset and duration of otitis media with effusion in the first two years of life," *J Pediatr*, 1993, Vol. 123, 702–711.

3. Maroeska, "Is pacifier use a risk factor for acute otitis media? A dynamic cohort study," *Family Practice*, 2008, Vol. 25, issue 4, 233–236.

4. McCormick, D.P., et al., "Non-severe acute otitis media: a clinical trial comparing outcomes of watchful waiting versus immediate antibiotic treatment," *Pediatrics*, June 2005, Vol. 115, issue 6, 1455.

5. *Pediatrics, Official Journal of the American Academy of Pediatrics*, June 2005, Vol. 115, Issue 6, June 2005, 1466–1473 (doi:10.1542/peds.2004-1473).

6. U.S. Department of Health and Human Services, Management of Acute Otitis Media, Evidence Report/Technology Assessment: Number 15, *AHRQ Publication Number 00-E008*.

7. Bezakova, N., R.A.M.J. Damoiseaux, A.W. Hoes, et al., "Recurrence up to 3.5 years after antibiotic treatment of acute otitis media in very young Dutch children: survey of trial participants," *BMJ*, 2009, Issue 339, b2525.

8. January 2009 issue of the *Archives of Disease in Childhood*, 2008, Issue 93, 40–44.

9. Pediatric Academic Societies (PAS) 2009 Annual Meeting: Abstract 4525.7. Presented May 4, 2009. *PAS 2009: Pediatric Tympanostomy Tube Use Steadily Rising; Trend Shows Significant Overuse.*

15

Fever

"Give me a fever and I can cure the child."
—HIPPOCRATES

THERE IS A STRONG MOTIVATION to *do something* when your child is not feeling well. Fever probably makes parents anxious more than almost any other common condition. Parents fear fever not only because it makes their child look and feel ill, but also because they're concerned that the fever means there is a serious medical problem underlying the fever, or that the fever is going to harm their child. The majority of calls to pediatricians are related to fevers in children.

Historically, due to more serious illnesses of the past, fevers were indeed potentially devastating and, if old movies are any guide, a fever was something that could lead to catastrophic outcomes short of a dramatic breaking of the fever at dawn.

Fear of fever remains part of the collective consciousness because in our modern age there is still so much advertising for fever-reducing medications such as Tylenol, and physician's offices readily give samples and dosage advice for these drugs. It stands to reason that it must be necessary to take steps to abolish the fever, even waking a peacefully sleeping child to do so.

217

> *A fever represents a universal, ancient, and usually beneficial response to infection. It is one of the body's most effective weapons for fighting disease.*

Actually, *a fever represents a universal, ancient, and usually beneficial response to infection.* It is one of the body's most effective weapons for fighting disease. Usually the best thing you can do is to let the fever run its course and do its job. There have been enough scientific studies over the years to show that fever is not harmful and that lowering fever may prolong an illness.

Fever helps defend against infection. Interfering with the process may do more harm than good.

What a Fever Is, What It Isn't

Just what is a fever and what does it do? Fever is not an illness. It is an elevation in body temperature, usually in response to a viral or bacterial infection. When an illness is detected, a part of the brain called the hypothalamus increases the body's metabolism while decreasing its ability to disperse heat.

A fever:

- makes it very difficult for infections to thrive because illness-causing germs will likely not survive in the higher temperature;
- reduces the amount of iron in the bloodstream that's needed by the invading virus or bacteria, thus starving the infection of needed nutrients; and
- increases the activity of white blood cells that kill bacteria in the body.

The makers of such drugs as Tylenol (acetaminophen) and Motrin (ibuprofen) certainly want you to believe that fever is something that ought to be suppressed whenever it occurs. However, because fever helps the body combat viruses and bacteria by retarding their growth

OTC DRUGS CAN BE MANUFACTURED UNSAFELY

Yet another reason to wonder about the wisdom about giving such over-the-counter products like Tylenol and Motrin to infants and children is that defects in the manufacturing process can render these products unsafe. For instance, in May 2010, McNeil Consumer Healthcare (a unit of Johnson & Johnson) was forced by the FDA to recall all liquid formulations of Tylenol and Motrin for babies and children. According to the manufacturer, there were various problems with these formulations, including the presence of foreign particles such as metal specks, unlabeled inactive ingredients, or more of the active ingredient than was on the label. A McNeil Consumer Healthcare release stated, "As a precautionary measure, parents and caregivers should not administer these products to their children."

> *When infant and child medications are recalled, these announcements often fail to reach the millions of families that have these products in their medicine cabinet.*

When infant and child medications are recalled, these announcements often fail to reach the millions of families that have these products in their medicine cabinet. There is currently no process in place for consumers to be contacted directly by manufacturers about product recalls.

and by stimulating an immunological response, reaching for a drug to bring down a child's fever may delay recovery. A growing body of research shows that letting a fever run its course may reduce the length and severity of such illnesses as colds, the flu, and other viral syndromes. In studies of children with routine infection, those who were treated with antipyretics (fever reducers) stayed sick longer.

In most cases, it is not even necessary to take your child's temperature. It is enough to identify by touch whether your child feels warm. The actual number of his temperature is of little importance because the degree of fever is not related to the severity of the child's illness. A very ill-appearing child with a fever of 101°F would be much more of a concern than a child who feels fine, is drinking and playing, but has a fever of 105°F. Children with a fever who are acting normally rarely have a serious medical problem.

Fever Phobia

The term "fever phobia" was coined in 1980 by Dr. Barton D. Schmitt, a pediatrician at the University of Colorado Medical Center in Denver, who found in a study that parents were often unduly concerned about fever and overreacted to it.

Twenty years later, in 2000, researchers at Johns Hopkins Medical Center in Baltimore undertook a study[1] to revisit parental attitudes toward fever. Results showed that concerns about fever and its potential harmful effects persisted, and that such concerns may lead to parental behaviors such as excessive monitoring and treatment.

Excessive and Intrusive

More than half of those interviewed in the Johns Hopkins study said that they would check a temperature every hour or less when their child had a fever, and 85 percent of caregivers said that they would awaken their child to give fever reducers during a febrile illness. According to the authors, frequently taking a child's temperature is neither necessary nor desirable, and waking a child to give fever-reducing medicine is rarely warranted: "These behaviors may be considered excessive and intrusive to children during the time that they are recovering from their illness."

Ninety-one percent of caregivers in the Johns Hopkins study believed that fever could have life-threatening or lethal effects. Twenty-one percent listed brain damage as the number one harmful effect of fever and 14 percent listed death. The authors point out that many

FEBRILE SEIZURES

A small percentage (about 3 percent) of children have an underlying predisposition that causes them to have a brief seizure when their temperature *rises at an extremely rapid rate.* The seizures are brief and are not harmful in any way. Most children who have this type of seizure will never have another one. Most children (97 percent) will never have a seizure, no matter how high their fever goes or how quickly it rises.

These seizures, or febrile convulsions, usually occur at the very beginning of an illness before the parents even realize that there is a fever. For this reason, aggressively treating fever does not prevent seizures.

The first time a seizure happens is understandably terrifying to parents, but children who experience febrile convulsions are no more likely to develop epilepsy than children who have no previous history of them. The very small percentage of children who experience convulsions do not have any after-effects. The seizures, if they do occur, most often happen between the ages of six months and 3 years.

The seizure, characterized by jerking body movements and twitching, generally lasts less than five minutes. The reason that some children have this susceptibility isn't well understood. Family history or previous occurrence increases the likelihood of seizure. Simple febrile seizures are self-limited and harmless. If your child has a seizure, try to stay calm, keep the environment around your child safe, and allow the seizure to resolve spontaneously without restraint.

The most common cause of febrile seizures is a viral illness called roseala, a benign childhood disease characterized by high fever (104°F degrees is common). The fever often ends abruptly after three to five days, at about the same time that a rash appears on the child's trunk and spreads over the body. One characteristic of roseala is that the child does not act particularly ill even when the fever is quite elevated. Roseala is most common during the "age of teething," between six months and 2 years. It is around six months that the maternal antibodies gained while in the womb begin to wear off, and that most breast-feeding children begin consuming formula or solid foods, reducing the full protectiveness that only exclusive breast milk can bring. This is why babies tend to develop their first illness around the middle of their first year.

---

of these beliefs also may be shared by pediatric healthcare providers. They discuss another study[2] that found that 65 percent of pediatricians who responded to a questionnaire believed that an elevated body temperature in and of itself could become dangerous to a child. Sixty percent of these physicians cited a temperature of 40°C (104°F) or above as significant. When asked about the most serious complication of fever, 21 percent listed brain damage and 26 percent listed death.

No scientific tests or investigations have ever confirmed the common fear that fever could cause brain damage. In the rare cases of meningitis or encephalitis, though, the opposite is true. These conditions themselves cause brain damage, which can then interfere with the brain's ability to control the body's temperature. In neurologically normal children, the brain has an internal regulatory mechanism that does not allow fever to rise out of control. Fevers produced by viral or bacterial infections will not cause brain damage or permanent physical harm, despite the myths about children being severely compromised by having a high fever.

> No scientific tests or investigations have ever confirmed the common fear that fever could cause brain damage.

Fever and Newborns

Parents are advised to seek medical help when a fever arises in a newborn during the first two months, as there is a heightened level of concern in such a young baby. Breast-feeding plays a critical role here, as breast-fed babies are protected from a vast range of illnesses and have a lesser risk of developing febrile illnesses in the newborn phase.

Home Treatment

When a fever occurs, it is not necessary to artificially lower the temperature. It is, however, important to have the child drink plenty of fluids, because during this time of elevated body temperature, it's easy to become dehydrated. Signs of dehydration can be difficult to detect in young infants, but they include dryness of the mucous membranes (dry lips, lack of tears), dry skin, infrequent wet diapers, and a sunken fontanel (soft spot on the skull).

Encourage children to drink plenty of water or at least sips of water at frequent intervals. Honey or lemon can be added to the water and you can offer diluted fresh juice as well. Breast milk is perfect for nursing infants and will probably be all that is wanted anyway.

Store-bought commercial electrolyte-replacing solutions (Pedialyte) are expensive and unnecessary. They are mixtures of sugar, salt, and water with some potassium. Instead, juice pops, soup broth, and herbal teas are excellent choices to replace electrolytes used up in the fever process. Older babies or young children may be reluctant to drink, so sucking on ice cubes, frozen juice, or

> *Store-bought commercial electrolyte-replacing solutions (Pedialyte) are expensive and unnecessary. They are mixtures of sugar, salt, and water with some potassium. Instead, juice pops, soup broth, and herbal teas are excellent choices to replace electrolytes used up in the fever process.*

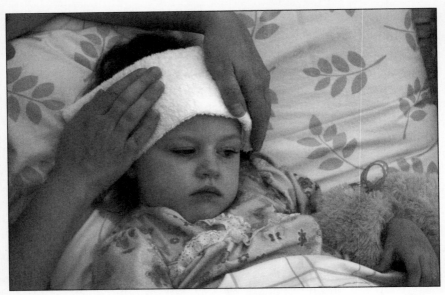

iStock

Fevers probably make parents anxious more than almost any other common condition. Rest during times of fever allows the body to use its energy to fight off infection.

a wet cloth or sponge may be an effective alternative. Rest during times of fever allows the body to use its energy to fight off infection.

Don't be too concerned if a feverish child does not want to eat. It is common for children with an elevated temperature not to have an appetite, so don't insist. This reduced appetite is a good sign, actually, as fasting helps the body to further eliminate toxins and allows the body's energy to focus on recovery, rather than digestion. Encourage a hungry child to eat light wholesome meals that are easily digested like vegetable soup, or raw or stewed fruit.

How your child looks is more important than the exact reading on the thermometer. As noted, children with a fever who are acting "like themselves" rarely have a serious medical problem. The illness is probably not serious if your child is alert and interested in his surroundings, is drinking fluids, and generally seems well. No treatment is needed other than fluids and rest.

The World Health Organization's Oral Rehydration Solution works just as well as Pedialyte and for a tiny fraction of the cost. Plus, it consists of readily available ingredients. It is for babies six months or older.

Table salt (NaCl)	½ teaspoon
Salt substitute (KCl)	½ teaspoon
Baking soda	½ teaspoon
Table sugar	2 tablespoons

Mix all in one liter (one quart plus two tablespoons) of boiled water. Cool thoroughly before giving it to your baby. Store solution in the refrigerator and throw away leftover solution after one week. This tastes quite salty to someone who isn't dehydrated.

During those times when a high fever becomes uncomfortable enough to cause your child to be sleepy and glassy eyed, this is just nature's way of keeping the body resting in bed so that all resources and energies can be diverted to getting well. The child may even talk nonsense, become twitchy, or experience hallucinations, irritability, and confusion when suffering from very high fever. In this case a cold washcloth to the head can cool the brain down a bit without interrupting the infection fighting ability of the fever.

Deciding to Call the Doctor

Fever is a natural process, but any time that you feel concerned, asking your pediatrician to evaluate your child for a possible serious infection is reasonable and expected. A child with a fever might have an underlying illness that needs to be diagnosed and possibly treated, so *advice to let a fever run its course is not the same as ignoring*

Fever is nature's way of keeping the child rested.

what might be a serious condition if there is something else about your child's condition that doesn't seem right to you. Your pediatrician will look for the possible source of fever, ask questions about your child's illness, and do a thorough exam.

A fever is more likely to be associated with a serious illness if there are major changes in appearance and behavior or other additional symptoms.

Call your child's doctor if:

- Your baby is under two months old and has a fever. Infants do not fight infections very well. Because of this your doctor will be more worried about your infant if he has a fever.
- An older child is persistently warm and does not respond to home treatment within three days.
- The fever is associated with respiratory difficulty. Look for labored breathing while your child's at rest, or noisy breathing.
- The baby or child refuses to drink or breast-feed (there is a risk of dehydration).
- Your child is always lying down—even after the fever has dropped—and does not want to play and drink fluids (there might be a more serious, underlying illness).
- There are associated symptoms such as irritability (difficult to console), abdominal pain, limping, or pain during urination.

Now you know . . .

Traditional wisdom and contemporary research suggest that suppressing fever is not necessarily health promoting and, in fact, may even be harmful.

FOOTNOTES

1. "Fever Phobia Revisited: Have Parental Misconceptions About Fever Changed in 20 Years?" *Pediatrics*, June 2001, Vol. 107, Issue 6, 1241–1246.
2. A. May and H. Bauchner, "Fever phobia. The pediatrician's contribution," *Pediatrics*, 1992, Vol. 90, 851–854.

16

Natural Healing vs. Medications

"The art of medicine consists of keeping the patient amused while nature heals the disease."
—Voltaire (1694–1778)

"One of the first duties of the physician is to educate the masses not to take medicine."
—Sir William Osler,
Nineteeth century British physician

"We chat together; he gives me prescriptions; I never follow them so I get well."
—Moliere

IT'S HARD TO HAVE YOUR CHILD GET SICK, and it is natural to seek the advice of a medical professional when it happens.

Yet when parents make frequent trips to the doctor, requesting medications for everyday aches and pains and common ailments such as colds, they teach children that there is a drug for every malady, for every age, and for every medical condition.

Medical doctors often intervene in processes which, if given time, would totally cure the patient without the doctor's assistance.

There is not "a pill for everything," and the doctor is not part of every cure.

Doctors are not taught to wait and see if things get better. They are not taught to have faith in the body's amazing ability to heal itself. Rather, physicians are taught to rely on expensive and dangerous tests and drugs, such as antibiotics, cold medications, and fever reducers, most of which interrupt the natural healing process and often make the patient's condition worse in the long run.

Over-the-counter (OTC) and prescription drugs are, in general terms, complex unnatural chemical compounds that very often are given to encourage the human body to act in a way in which it was not designed and that rarely addresses the underlying problem. Most of these drugs are taxing to the liver, kidneys, and/or other systems of the body.

> *When parents make frequent trips to the doctor, requesting medications for everyday aches and pains and common ailments such as colds, they teach children that there is a drug for every malady, for every age, and for every medical condition. But there is not "a pill for everything," and the doctor is not part of every cure.*

Unfortunately, the increased marketing by drug companies directly to consumers, unheard of in years past, has created a climate of media-driven demand for drugs that are not always appropriate. Even physicians agree that antibiotics and other medications are over-used, but pediatricians sometimes feel pressure by parents to prescribe something when they really know that the condition will disappear in a few days without medical intervention.

Some medical conditions do require immediate conventional care, as in the case of a severe asthma attack, but with most other conditions and symptoms you can take a wait-and-see attitude while you pursue natural methods that do not involve a risk of side effects.

Even when your pediatrician discovers a medical problem, you can still investigate alternatives to conventional treatment. If you have found a doctor who respects your desire to pursue the most natural and gentle forms of treatment possible, you can communicate openly, utilizing your pediatrician for diagnostic information and discussing options for your child.

Coughs and Colds

After years of pediatricians pushing cold medication, the American Academy of Pediatrics (AAP) now recognizes contemporary research and recommends against medicating young children to treat cold symptoms—a belated acknowledgment that these products are ineffective and unsafe. The symptoms of a cold are self-limiting and benign for most people who experience them.

In 2007, the Food and Drug Administration (FDA) advisory panel recommended a ban on OTC cough and cold medicine intended for children under age 6. The FDA also issued a Public Health Advisory for parents and caregivers, recommending that OTC cough and cold products should not be used to treat infants and children under 2 because serious and potentially life-threatening side effects can occur from using these medicines, something that aware health practitioners and enlightened parents have known for decades.

Wyeth, a major OTC drug manufacturer wrote to physicians: "We voluntarily removed our 'Infant Dimetapp' and Robitussin products from the market to help reduce the potential for dosing errors and overdoses in children, who are most vulnerable to serious outcomes resulting from the misuse of cough and cold medications."

Every week, one out of ten American children still use OTC cough and cold medications—usually a combination of at least two types of medications, including antihistamines, cough suppressants, expectorants, decongestants, and fever reducers.[1] This is despite the FDA and AAP recommendations against using them, and also despite the fact that not one OTC remedy has ever been found to be more

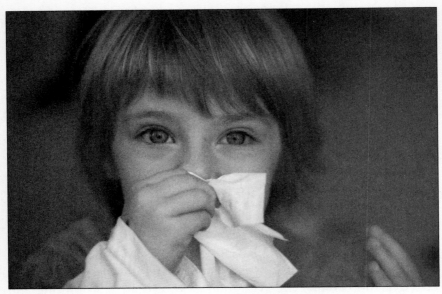

iStock

Cough and cold products are ineffective and unsafe. Alternatively, foods with high levels of vitamin C and zinc make good remedies.

effective than placebos in eliminating cough and cold symptoms. And, as mentioned, many of these OTC drugs can have dangerous side effects. Further, as mentioned in Chapter 15, fever is an important immune system mechanism, the suppression of which is known to prolong the very illness for which the child is being treated.

There are things that you can do, at home, to provide relief for cold symptoms in a safe manner. Saline (a simple salt solution) nose spray and drops help with irritation of nasal passages. This works particularly well in conjunction with nasal suction bulbs. The simple act of keeping the child's head elevated, especially during sleep, can significantly reduce the pressure on the sinuses and nasal passages.

Cool mist humidifiers can decrease the irritation of the upper airway (although be mindful of a humidifier's ability, as mentioned in Chapter 12, to exacerbate dust mite population growth). Vapor rubs are popular, age-old remedies, too, but be aware of the possibility of accidental ingestion. Critical for cold relief at home is ensuring that your child gets plenty of fluids.

Given bed rest and wholesome food, the body heals itself from colds with no need for antihistamines, decongestants, or fever-lowering drugs. Colds and viruses, just like fevers, are a part of life and a way for the immune system to respond appropriately to avoid future infections. Keeping the child comfortable is all that is required while letting nature run its course.

More Cold Remedies

Vitamin C and zinc are two home remedies that are already familiar to many parents.

Foods high in vitamin C, which, as mentioned in the nutrition chapter, acts as an antioxidant and assists the body in producing the connective tissue component collagen, include berries, broccoli, cantaloupe, carrots, green beans, honeydew melon, orange, papaya, peaches, peas, romaine lettuce, spinach, strawberries, sweet potatoes, and tomatoes.

As noted in Chapter 13, zinc is a mineral critical for maintaining proper immune function and skin health. Zinc-rich foods include poultry, baked potato, brown rice, lentils, oatmeal, peas, salmon, spinach, whole wheat bread, and yogurt.

Ear Infections

Ear infections, as observed in Chapter 14, are the number-one reason why parents bring their children to the pediatrician. You now know that 80 percent to 90 percent of correctly diagnosed ear infections will clear up on their own, yet doctors continue to write millions of unnecessary prescriptions for them annually. As noted, the drugs in many cases may lead to side effects, hard-to-treat and recurring infection, and a resistance to antibiotics.

Equally problematic, when antibiotics kill bacteria, they may also kill many of the beneficial microflora in the intestines at the same time. When these "good bacteria" are wiped out, as described in the ear infections chapter, the child can suffer from gastrointestinal problems like yeast overgrowth and diarrhea.

POSITIVE EFFECTS OF HONEY

Honey is an example of a natural, more effective, and safer alternative to over-the-counter cough medicines.

- In a study reported in the December 2007 issue of *The Archives of Pediatric and Adolescent Medicine*,[2] a single nighttime dose (thirty minutes before bedtime) of one or two teaspoons of buckwheat honey was clearly effective in reducing cough frequency and severity, as well as improving the sleep quality for children and parents. Dextromethorphan (DM, the main ingredient in OTC cough medications) was not any better than no treatment at all and had no effect on the cough. The authors conclude that "Honey may be a preferable treatment for the cough and sleep difficulty associated with childhood upper respiratory tract infection."
- Honey has well-established antioxidant and antimicrobial effects, and it might be that sweet substances of any kind help dissolve mucus in the airways and soothe the back of the throat. Honey is not recommended for children under 1 year because there have been rare cases of infants getting botulism from ingesting honey. Children older than one do not face this risk.

It is not only the individual child taking the antibiotic who is harmed. For society as a whole, overuse of antibiotics is a major public health problem. As a result of natural selection and mutations, resistant strains of bacteria can thrive within individuals and then spread throughout the population, eventually rendering most antibiotics useless.

"Resistance," as described by the World Health Organization:[3]

Microbes (the collective term for bacteria, fungi, parasites, and viruses) cause infectious diseases, and antimicrobial agents, such as penicillin, streptomycin, and more than 150 others, have been developed to combat the spread and severity of many of these diseases. Resistance to antimicrobials is a natural biological phenomenon that can be amplified or accelerated by a variety of factors, including human practices. The use of an antimicrobial for any infection, real or feared, in any dose and over any time period, forces microbes to either adapt or die in a phenomenon known as "selective pressure." The microbes which adapt and survive carry genes for resistance, which can be passed on.

Pediatricians, who might be diligent in treating a child's ear infections once they occur, seldom discuss with parents what might be causing a child's recurring ear infections in the first place and what steps can be taken to prevent them. A common result is that the parents continue to bring the child in for repeated ear infections and multiple courses of antibiotics. Frustrated parents are then told that the child may be a candidate for the surgically-inserted tympanostomy tubes (described in Chapter 14). In some cases the child already has these tubes but is continuing to get the ear infections because proper attention has not been paid to the underlying cause.

> It is not only the individual child taking the antibiotic who is harmed. For society as a whole, overuse of antibiotics is a major public health problem. As a result of natural selection and mutations, resistant strains of bacteria can thrive within individuals and then spread throughout the population, eventually rendering most antibiotics useless.

Croup

If your child suddenly wakes up in the middle of the night with noisy breathing and a "barking seal" cough, it can be terrifying. Croup (*laryngotracheobronchitis*) is a viral infection that causes swelling centered at the larynx (vocal cords). It tends to occur in children around the "age of teething" (between six months and 2 years). The cough invariably gets worse at night, usually around 2 A.M.

As the cough gets more frequent, the child may have stridor, a noisy sound when inhaling air through a swollen larynx. Exposing your child to cool moist air can briefly decrease the swelling in the larynx and improve the symptoms. Because the cool outside night air often temporarily cures the condition, panicky parents can "pretend to go to the emergency room," that is, get in the car, roll down the windows and drive to the nearest hospital.

By the time you and your child arrive at the ER, the croup is often much improved and you can all go home. Chances are, though, the process will occur again the next night and maybe a few more nights after that. Other remedies are to briefly put the child's face near the open freezer door, or to keep a cool-mist humidifier close to the bed to decrease swelling of the larynx. An older remedy of going into the bathroom and steaming it up with a hot shower can provide some relief, although cool mist is better than steam in this instance.

Fortunately, croup is almost never life threatening, but always remember to trust your instincts. Call your pediatrician if you're uncomfortable with your child's condition. And seek medical attention for your child immediately if after thirty minutes of any of these mist treatments his breathing hasn't improved, he's struggling to breathe, has persistent stridor at rest, or retractions (an inward pulling of the muscles between the ribs during the inhaling phase of breathing so that the ribs become prominent), is drooling, or seems unusually agitated.

Roseala

As noted in Chapter 15, the viral illness roseala commonly causes unusually high fevers. Like croup, it usually occurs in children between six months and two years. Because of the rapid rise of temperature at the onset of the illness, a small percentage of children initially experience a febrile seizure. The fever fluctuates around 103 degrees for three or four days and swollen lymph glands typically appear at the base of the scalp in the back of the head. The child is usually just mildly irritable, with some eye rubbing as if his eyes are uncomfortable, but the child usually does not seem ill in proportion to the height of the temperature. The illness is self-limited—it runs its course—and does not require treatment.

Probiotics for Prevention

As discussed in previous chapters, probiotics, microscopic living organisms that are mixtures of beneficial bacteria, help to maintain the natural balance of organisms (microflora) in the intestines. The results of a 2009 international study[4] reported in *Pediatrics* suggest that children who take probiotics experience significantly fewer cold and flu symptoms than children who do not take them.

The largest group of probiotic bacteria in the intestine is lactic acid bacteria; the best known of these is *Lactobacillus acidophilus*. Children ages 3 to 5 who consumed a special milk containing two kinds of probiotic bacteria (*Lactobacillus acidophilus* along with *Bifidobacterium animalis*) developed 72 percent fewer fevers, 62 percent fewer episodes of cough, and 59 percent fewer runny noses. These children were also 32 percent less likely to miss days of school than the children who drank plain milk. All the children who took the probiotics were up to 84 percent less likely to need antibiotics as well. Some health professionals recommend that every time a child is given antibiotics, he should be given probiotics afterwards in order to restore the beneficial gut microflora that the medicine eliminates.

The probiotics are generally safe and well tolerated and are found in sources other than altered milk. Foods that contain probiotics include sauerkraut, yogurt, miso, tempeh, and some specifically manufactured fruit juice beverages. Probiotic supplements also are available in capsules, tablets, and powders.

Rather than use unnecessary medications that often mask symptoms, interfere with immunity, or have damaging side effects, you can take steps to promote the strength of your child's immune system and avoid the things that can weaken it:

- Breast-feed your baby. Breast-feeding supports a healthy immune system.
- Feed your child the highest quality foods available to support immune function, including using organic whole foods when possible and avoiding packaged ones that contain partially hydrogenated fats, nitrates, corn syrup, preservatives, and artificial colors.
- Eliminate chemicals and allergens. Use natural soaps, shampoos, and laundry products. Avoid exposure to harsh cleaning products, cigarette smoke, and insecticides.
- Ensure that your child spends plenty of time outdoors getting healthy exercise and adequate exposure to sunshine so that he can obtain sufficient levels of vitamin D.

> *Rather than use unnecessary medications that often mask symptoms, interfere with immunity, or have damaging side effects, you can take steps to promote the strength of your child's immune system and avoid the things that can weaken it.*

In every situation, whether you elect to give your child medication of not, he will certainly benefit from the lifestyle changes suggested in this chapter.

Now you know . . .

The vast majority of children with viral infections will get better on their own and will get better faster without drug treatments.

FOOTNOTES

1. A.E. Shefrin et al., *Can Fam Physician*, November 2009, Vol. 55, Issue 11, 1081–1083.
2. Ian Paul, M.D., M.Sc., December 2007, *Archives of Pediatrics and Adolescent Medicin.*, Penn State College of Medicine.
3. World Health Organization, Fact Sheet No.194, Revised January 2002.
4. Gregory J. Leyer, Ph.D., Li Shuguang, M.S., Mohamed E. Mubasher, Ph.D., Cheryl Reifer, Ph.D., and Arthur C. Ouwehand, Ph.D., "Effects on Cold and Influenza-Like Symptom Incidence and Duration in Children," August 2009, *Pediatrics*, Vol. 124, Issue 2, e172–e179.

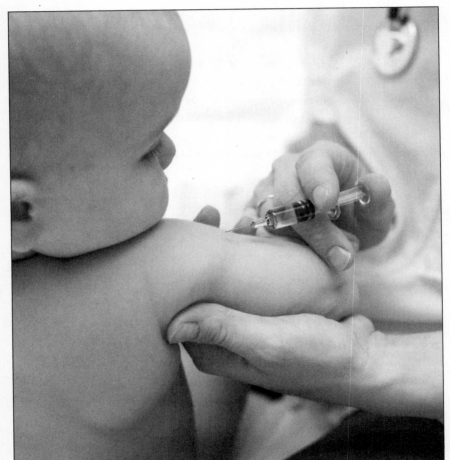

17

Vaccinations:
Every Vaccine Has a Story

PARENTS ARE INCREASINGLY becoming concerned at the U.S. government's push to "have your child vaccinated or else." Some parents may be philosophically opposed, believing that vaccines go against their core beliefs about health and wellness. Some may object to what seems to be a painful assault on their child, while other parents may feel that the benefits of immunization do not justify the risks. As more and more childhood vaccines are offered, parents are getting more concerned about what seems to be a harsh overload on a child's young body.

While the welfare of your child is paramount, parents and health professionals may not always agree on what's in the best interests of each individual child. It is not the purpose of this chapter to tell you whether or not to vaccinate but to analyze and evaluate the story behind each vaccine. The goal here is to point out some reasons why you should examine the facts before deciding whether or not to submit your child to some or all of the recommended vaccines.

The medical establishment considers vaccines effective if they suppress a few targeted illnesses—but at what expense? Although most children have no immediate adverse reaction to the vaccines, it does not necessarily follow that there is nothing to worry about.

An emerging body of evidence indicates that vaccines can damage a child's developing immune system and brain, leading to debilitating and life-threatening disorders like attention deficit disorders, asthma, allergies, and other conditions, many of which barely existed before mass vaccination programs.

The thinking behind universal vaccination is that it lessens risks across populations for any given disease. Well-meaning nurses, doctors, and school staffers often gently coerce parents to conform to the notion that vaccination is a standard procedure. Don't all parents want to keep their children healthy and spare them from serious diseases? So when we're told that we should have our children vaccinated for fifteen different diseases during their infancy, most parents readily do so. It is hard to resist, especially for vulnerable first-time parents or those who have been brought up in a medical environment.

However, we're talking about your baby, and you need to be part of the decisions. You owe it to your child to make informed decisions based on facts, not bullying tactics. If you feel you're being pressured by a medical professional to vaccinate your child and are unsure of what to do, the best answer is "Thank you. I will do some more reading on this and let you know my decision."

> If you feel you're being pressured by a medical professional to vaccinate your child and are unsure of what to do, the best answer is "Thank you. I will do some more reading on this and let you know my decision."

Many pediatricians, not all, are unwilling or unable to discuss this subject calmly or with an open mind. They are part of the medical establishment, in alliance with the Centers for Disease Control and Prevention (CDC) and the pharmaceutical companies, so their personal and professional identities are based upon the assumed effectiveness and safety of vaccines.

Even the United States government has recently acknowledged a problem related to the presumed safety of vaccines. In December of

2009 the Department of Health and Human Services revealed that many of the experts hired by the CDC for advice on vaccines had not disclosed ethical violations related to conflicts of interest.[1] They were in fact being paid by drug companies with an interest in their decisions. These so-called experts hired by the CDC were potentially recommending vaccines—even ones they know to be unsafe—in part because the manufacturers were paying them.

The American Academy of Pediatrics (AAP), which strongly endorses universal immunization, acknowledges that physicians may need to tolerate parental decisions with which they disagree if those decisions are not likely to be harmful to the child. Parents are free to make choices regarding medical care unless those choices place their child at substantial risk of serious harm.

In an AAP survey, a small number of pediatricians reported that they always (4.8 percent) or sometimes (18.1 percent) tell parents that they will no longer serve as the child's physician if, after educational efforts, the parents continue to refuse permission for an immunization.

The AAP Committee on Bioethics has published information for pediatricians when parents refuse immunizations. Its publication, *Responding to Parental Refusals of Immunization of Children*, was initially published in May 2005[2] and then a statement of reaffirmation for this policy was published in May 2009. In one section of this publication, the Academy discusses that the parental refusal of vaccines might be contrary to community interest and might jeopardize the public health:

A parent's refusal to immunize his or her child also raises an important question of justice that has been described as the problem of "free riders." Parents who refuse immunization on behalf of their children are, in a sense, free riders who take advantage of the benefit created by the participation and assumption of immunization risk or burden by others while refusing to participate in the program themselves. The decision to refuse to immunize a child is made less risky because others have created an environment in which herd immunity will likely keep the unimmunized child safe. These individuals place family interest ahead of civic responsibility. Although such parents do reject what many would consider to be a moral duty, coercive measures to require immunization of a child over parental objections are justified only in cases in which others are placed at substantial risk of serious harm by the parental decision.

Compulsory [forced] immunization laws in the United States have been upheld repeatedly as a reasonable exercise of the state's police power in the absence of an epidemic or even a single case. They also have been found to be constitutional even for cases in which the laws conflict with the religious beliefs of individuals . . .

In a highly immunized population in which disease prevalence is low, the risk of disease from the small number of children who remain unimmunized does not usually pose a significant-enough health risk to others to justify state action. Diseases with very high morbidity and mortality (such as smallpox), however, might create a situation in which even a single case of infection would justify mandatory immunization of the population. For most routine vaccines, less forcible alternatives can be used justifiably to encourage parents to immunize children because of the public health benefit. In the case of vaccines routinely recommended for children, the AAP supports the use of appropriate public health measures, education, and incentives for immunization. Because unimmunized children do pose a risk to other children who lack immunity to vaccine-preventable infections, the AAP also supports immunization requirements for school entry.

When parents read, as above, that "compulsory immunization laws in the United States have been upheld repeatedly as a reasonable exercise of the state's police power in the absence of an epidemic or even a single case," there might be some confusion about vaccinations and the requirements for school entrance. It is actually quite simple. Although each state has laws addressing recommended childhood immunizations prior to school entry, vaccination is not strictly mandatory. You do not have to vaccinate your children so they can attend school. They all have provisions for parents to sign a waiver stating that all or some of the vaccines have not been given because of medical, personal, or religious reasons. Parents have the absolute right to determine whether or not their child receives vaccinations, and it is not legal to interfere with that right.

The AAP publication ends with advice to pediatricians about how to respond to parents who refuse immunizations for their children:

> What is the pediatrician to do when faced with a parent who refuses immunization for his or her child? First and most important, the pediatrician should listen carefully and respectfully to the parent's concerns, recognizing that some parents may not use the same decision criteria as the physician and may weigh evidence very differently than the physician does. Vaccines are very safe, but they are not risk free; nor are they 100 percent effective. This poses a dilemma for many parents and should not be minimized. The pediatrician should share honestly what is and is not known about the risks and benefits of the vaccine in question, attempt to understand the parent's concerns about immunization, and attempt to correct any misperceptions and misinformation.

You do not have to vaccinate your children so they can attend school. They all have provisions for parents to sign a waiver stating that all or some of the vaccines have not been given because of medical, personal, or religious reasons. Parents have the absolute right to determine whether or not their child receives vaccinations, and it is not legal to interfere with that right.

Continued refusal after adequate discussion should be respected unless the child is put at significant risk of serious harm (as, for example, might be the case during an epidemic). Only then should state agencies be involved to override parental discretion on the basis of medical neglect.

Adverse Reactions

Some children have had bad reactions to vaccines involving very high fevers, seizures, and other problems. Some of these reactions are severe enough to suggest that giving another dose of that same vaccine ought to be prohibited. Other reactions might not—from a purely medical point of view—mean that another dose should not be given, but parents may prefer to be cautious and skip the rest of that particular vaccination series.

The First Months

The hepatitis B vaccine was discussed in the first chapter. It is very unlikely a child will contract or spread hepatitis B. The virus is spread by coming in contact with the blood of infected persons, most of whom are considered to be in "high risk groups." These groups include adults who inject illegal drugs with contaminated needles, or are chronic alcoholics, or are sexually promiscuous individuals (homosexual or heterosexual) who have been diagnosed with a sexually transmitted disease.

Hepatitis B is a liver disease caused by a virus. While a person can be quite ill with this infection, 50 percent will develop no symptoms and 30 percent develop only mild flu-like symptoms. Most patients recover within eight weeks without any long-term complications and likely will acquire lifetime immunity to the virus.

In 1991, the Advisory Committee of Immunization Practices (ACIP) began recommending the hepatitis B vaccine for newborns within the first forty-eight hours. Three separate doses are required. The government strategy is to eliminate the hepatitis B virus from the general population. Vaccination programs in the 1980s that had targeted high-risk groups did not work because many adults had refused the vaccine. Finding it difficult to vaccinate high risk groups with three doses of the vaccine, the government advisors decided the only way to control the problem was to vaccinate the entire population, starting at birth. Vaccine advocates emphasize that by starting at birth, right in the hospital, the pediatrician can avoid the newborn

This is a 1999 press release from the Association of American Physicians and Surgeons, Inc. Select portions have been italicized for emphasis by the author of this book.

July 8, 1999
FOR IMMEDIATE RELEASE:

DOCTORS CALL FOR MORATORIUM ON HEPATITIS B VACCINE FOR SCHOOLCHILDREN CITING POTENTIAL DEADLY OUTCOMES

School Districts Requiring Vaccines Accused of Practicing Medicine Without a License

The Association of American Physicians and Surgeons (AAPS) is calling for an immediate moratorium on mandatory hepatitis B vaccines for schoolchildren pending further research about dangerous side effects, and accused school districts that require the shots of practicing medicine without a license.

"Children younger than 14 are three times more likely to die or suffer adverse reactions after receiving hepatitis B vaccines than to catch the disease," said Jane M. Orient, M.D., Executive Director of AAPS. *"It's one thing to bar a student from school if he is carrying an infectious disease posing a threat to other children. But to require a questionable medical treatment as a condition of attendance crosses over the line to practicing medicine,"* said Dr. Orient.

In the U.S., Hepatitis B is primarily an adult disease, not spread by casual contact. Risk is highly dependent on lifestyle, i.e., multiple sex partners, drug abuse, or an occupation with exposure to blood. Yet the Centers for Disease Control and Prevention recommends all newborns be given this vaccine, and many school districts require it. Even state legislatures are guilty of this medical malpractice. For example, earlier this year, the Ohio state legislature passed a law requiring all schoolchildren to receive three doses of the vaccine.

According to a recent federal government study, serious adverse events after the vaccine—including 48 deaths—are reported three times as frequently as cases of hepatitis B in children under the age of 14. *"We suspect the adverse reactions are vastly underreported, as formal long-term studies of vaccine safety have not been completed,"* says Dr. Orient. *"We find it shocking that government health officials cavalierly dismiss reports of serious adverse vaccine effects as coincidental and that school officials ignore them altogether."*

In calling for the moratorium on hepatitis B mandates, Dr. Orient warns the increasing "vaccine cocktails" administered to children may be hazardous to their health. *"Mandates effectively use schoolchildren as research subjects subjected to unproved medical treatment without informed consent, in violation of the Nuremberg Code. If school administrators and government bureaucrats were subject to that code, they could be prosecuted as war criminals,"* says Dr. Orient.

"We suspect financial ties between vaccine manufacturers and medical groups such as the American Medical Association and American Academy of Pediatrics (AAP) which endorse the vaccine," says Dr. Orient, pointing to a substantial donation to AAP from Merck & Co. *"And the federal government pays the state a bonus up to $100 for every 'fully' vaccinated child. What's their motive—money or medicine?"*

A voice for private physicians since 1943, AAPS holds that the patient-physician relationship is inviolable and that parents, not government, should make decisions about their children's medical care.

encounter being a "missed opportunity"[3] of conveying to parents the importance of immunization. The pediatrician is encouraged to "lay the groundwork" for the routine schedule in infancy.[3]

If the hepatitis B vaccine is avoided or missed in the hospital at birth, then it is scheduled to be administered during the routine two-month office visit, along with five other vaccines:

- Inactivated Poliovirus [IPV] (three serotypes)
- *Haemophilus influenzae* type b conjugate vaccine [Hib]
- Pneumococcal conjugate vaccine [PCV] (*seven serotypes*)
- Diphtheria and tetanus toxoids and acellular pertussis (whooping cough) vaccine *[DTaP]*
- Rotavirus vaccine [RV] (four serotypes) {oral vaccine}

That is a total of five vaccines (composed of nineteen vaccine strains) and multiple doses of chemicals injected into an eight-week-old baby during the same visit. Vaccine ingredients are risky. They include dangerous preservatives and adjuvants (chemicals that increase immune response) and other potentially harmful substances, including aluminum phosphate, phenol (carbolic acid), MSG, formaldehyde (a known carcinogen), and gelatin. Toxins can accumulate and eventually suppress the immune system, cause brain damage, and lead to a myriad of health issues and developmental disorders. Exposure to toxins during the critical stages of development before age 2 is especially dangerous to the brain.

Parents are starting to question whether it's right to inject numerous different viruses and bacteria, mixed with a multitude of different chemicals and solvents, into babies' delicate, developing bodies to "protect" them.

It is important to investigate the risks of your baby acquiring hepatitis B and these other infections before you come for your infant's two-month well baby checkup, rather than being rushed into acquiescence at the time of your visit. You should be prepared with your questions and concerns. During the office visit you can tell your pediatrician which vaccines you feel are appropriate for your child and which you might prefer to postpone until your child's immune and

50 Vaccines by Age 5

By the time they go to kindergarten, children receive fifty vaccines (some in combination injections) against fifteen diseases.

Vaccine	Birth	1 month	2 months	4 months
			Age	
Hepatitis B	HepB	HepB		
Rotavirus			RV	RV
Diptheria, Tetanus, Pertussis			DTaP	DTaP
Haemophilus influenzae type b			Hib	Hib
Pneumococcal			PCV	PCV
Inactivated Poliovirus			IPV	IPV
Influenza				
Measles, Mumps, Rubella				
Varicella				
Hepatitis A				
Meningococcal				

50 Vaccines by Age 5 (continued)

Age						
6 months	12 months	15 months	18 months	19–23 months	2–3 years	4–6 years
HepB						
RV						
DTaP		DTaP			DTaP	
Hib	Hib					
PCV	PCV				PPSV	
IPV						IPV
Influenza (yearly)						
	MMR					MMR
	Varicella					Varicella
	HepA (2 doses)				HepA Series	
					MCV	

SOURCE: Centers for Disease Control and Prevention (CDC)

Range of recommended ages for all children except certain high-risk groups

Range of recommended certain high-risk groups

nervous systems are less susceptible to the potential toxic effects of the vaccine, at which point you'll make your decision about the postponed vaccines.

More Vaccines

In September 2009, new vaccine guidelines were issued by the expert panel of the Infectious Diseases Society of America (IDSA). It says, in part:

- New vaccines that have been licensed since 2002 include human papillomavirus vaccine; live, attenuated influenza vaccine; meningococcal conjugate vaccine; rotavirus vaccine; tetanus toxoid, reduced diphtheria toxoid, acellular pertussis vaccine; and zoster vaccine. New combination vaccines that have become available are measles, mumps, rubella, and varicella vaccine; tetanus, diphtheria, and pertussis and inactivated polio vaccine; and tetanus, diphtheria, and pertussis and inactivated polio/*Haemophilus influenzae* type b vaccine.
- For young children, hepatitis A vaccines are now universally recommended. All children aged six months through 18 years...should receive annual administration of influenza vaccines. The routine childhood and adolescent immunization schedule now includes a second dose of varicella vaccine. The adolescent and adult immunization schedules have expanded to accommodate many of these new recommendations.

The Varicella Vaccine

Chickenpox (*varicella*) is one of those childhood diseases that we used to hope everybody would actually catch in childhood to get it over with (before we had the vaccine). A study conducted by the CDC in 1985 determined that the vaccine was not necessary. However, in 1995 it was promoted as "cost-effective"—rather than essential—because parents would not have to miss work and stay home to care for their sick children. If working mothers could keep working instead of taking time off to care for their sick children, *businesses would save hundreds of millions of dollars.* The varicella vaccine was licensed shortly thereafter.

Before the vaccine was licensed, doctors would encourage parents to expose their children to the disease while they were young. That's because if caught during adulthood the disease can be much more severe and can entail many more complications that might require hospitalization. In young children, chickenpox is a relatively mild disease, especially compared to other diseases for which vaccines have been developed. Even the AAP advised in its 1996 brochure, "Most children who are otherwise healthy and get chickenpox won't have any complications from the disease."

As you can see, this vaccine was being touted for its economic benefits to business. This was the fist time that healthy children were vaccinated against a childhood disease that was largely benign (although, like any disease, there are rare instances of severe complications). Most children who contract natural varicella recover completely and have lifelong immunity. Sometimes the disease is so mild that an exposed child develops antibodies without the actual illness even being noticed.

When the chickenpox vaccine was originally developed, there was tremendous resistance from pediatricians, who knew that the disease is rarely dangerous and confers lifelong immunity. Many feared that the immunity gained by the vaccine would not be as good as that acquired through natural disease, and that when the vaccine wore off it would leave young adults vulnerable to infection. That is exactly what happened. Children's immunity was found to wane after several years. This then left the prospect of a future population of adults who had been vaccinated but whose immunity had declined enough to leave these individuals susceptible to even worse disease, and so it is now required that children get yet a second varicella vaccine before entering kindergarten. (The vaccine manufacturer of course gets double the profits.)

JOURNAL EXCERPTS USED DURING THE
CHICKENPOX VACCINE PROMOTION CAMPAIGN

Pediatrics, October 1986 (The official journal of the American Academy of Pediatrics)

The costs associated with a varicella infection in normal persons... have been estimated to be approximately $400 million (per year), 95 percent of which is the cost of caring for a child at home. Vaccination of normal 15-month-old children with a safe and effective vaccine with long-lasting immunity could reduce the cost by 66% and result in a savings of $7 for every dollar spent on the vaccination program. This assumes that vaccine would be administered only once with measles, mumps, and rubella vaccine [and] that there would be no increase in the number of varicella cases in older persons who are at increased risk for complications...

JAMA February 1994 (*Journal of the American Medical Association*)

OBJECTIVE: To evaluate the economic consequences of a routine varicella vaccination program that targets healthy children. RESULTS: A routine varicella vaccination program for healthy children would prevent 94 percent of all cases of chickenpox vaccine... It would cost approximately $162 million annually if one dose of vaccine per child were recommended at a cost of $35 per dose. From the societal perspective, which includes work-loss costs... the program would save more than $5 for every dollar invested in vaccination.

Fortune Magazine, April 4, 1994

Merck won't say how much vaccine each batch yields. A study commissioned by the Centers for Disease Control (CDC) suggests that a $162-million-a-year vaccination program would largely wipe out chickenpox in the U.S.; each dollar invested in the program, the study claims, would save society $5.40 in medical costs and hours of work lost by parents who stay home to nurse a sick child.

The Rubella Vaccine

Other than a rash, the adverse effects of rubella (German measles) for children are minimal: one-quarter to one-half of infections are *subclinical*, meaning that there are no symptoms and the illness goes undetected. For those who have symptoms, the condition lasts for about three to five days with fever, skin rash, and swollen glands. Most people make a complete recovery without complications. Vaccination against rubella has no clinical benefit for a child. Rubella vaccination is probably the only vaccination for a disease that is, in itself, probably less serious than the common cold.

The rubella virus in all batches of rubella vaccine made by Merck is descended from tissues obtained from an infected aborted fetus during the 1964 rubella epidemic, when many women were advised to terminate their pregnancies if the mothers contracted rubella.

If the only consequences of rubella were a few days of discomfort, there would be no need for a rubella vaccine. However, if a pregnant woman contracts the rubella infection during the first three months of pregnancy, this poses a risk to the unborn child, who could be born with congenital rubella syndrome (CRS), involving multiple congenital abnormalities.

Babies are vaccinated against rubella *only* because they are accessible. *The severe effects of rubella exposure on the unborn child make the rubella vaccine unique in that it is not given to protect the child who is being immunized.* We vaccinate all babies against rubella out of concern that a non-immune pregnant woman's unborn baby might be exposed. You might wonder why the campaign wasn't geared toward women wanting to become pregnant. The fact is, in some other countries, there is no universal immunization. Only young women of childbearing age who have not developed natural immunity (checked by a simple blood test) by the age of puberty are given the vaccine.

MMR

Until 2009, Merck had made available separate vaccines for measles, mumps, and rubella, so parents who objected to the tissue origin of the rubella vaccine on ethical grounds opted out of that particular one: the rubella virus in all batches of rubella vaccine made by Merck is descended from tissues obtained from an infected aborted fetus during the 1964 rubella epidemic, when many women were advised to terminate their pregnancies if the mothers contracted rubella. The rubella virus strain is RA 27/3. (RA stands for rubella abortion. The woman went to Sweden because the abortion was not legal in the United States at the time.)

Tetanus

Tetanus vaccination is unlike the others because tetanus is a disease that is not contagious—it does not spread from person to person. The vaccine is given to children as part of the combined the DTaP (diptheria, tetanus, and pertussis) vaccine. The toxin produced by the bacterium *Clostridium tetani* causes tetanus by entering the body through a wound. If public policy is designed to protect against broad threats to public health, then tetanus vaccination, which offers protection only to the individual receiving the vaccine, does not come under this mandate.

Gardasil

Yet another vaccine for perfectly healthy young girls: one of the recently marketed vaccines, Gardasil, is meant to cause immunity to certain genital warts—those caused by four particular strains of the human papilloma virus (HPV), allegedly the cause of cervical cancer. Merck & Co. promoted Gardasil primarily to "guard" against cervical cancer, rather than promoting it as a vaccine against HPV viruses or sexually transmitted diseases. The ubiquitous "One Less" campaign led girls and their mothers to feel empowered by getting this vaccine "against cancer," when HPV is really an extremely common

GARDASIL PACKAGE INSERT

GARDASIL is a vaccine indicated in girls and women nine to twenty-six years of age for the prevention of cervical, vulvar, and vaginal cancers; precancerous or dysplastic lesions; and genital warts caused by human papillomavirus (HPV) Types 6, 11, 16, and 18.

GARDASIL does not substitute for routine cervical cancer screening, and women who receive GARDASIL should continue to undergo screening.

---

virus that most people contract and get over rather quickly without incident.

In a few women, the HPV infection persists, and some women may develop precancerous cervical lesions, many of which resolve spontaneously. Some women eventually develop cancer, but it is impossible to predict the small percentage of women in which this is likely to occur.

The marketing of the vaccine was so successful that in its first year, Gardasil was named in the industry journal *Pharmaceutical Executive* as the "brand of the year" for building a "market out of thin air."

The vaccine was approved in 2006 for girls and young "women" ages 9 to 26 and is recommended for *routine vaccination* of girls 11 and 12.

HPV is transmitted by sexual contact. School children are not placed at significant risk for contracting HPV simply by virtue of being around unvaccinated individuals. In this way, HPV (like tetanus) strays from the initial reason for giving vaccines—stopping the transmission of highly infectious agents that were capable of infecting others through ordinary close contact.

Nine- to eleven-year-old girls inoculated with the vaccine will be adolescents when they pass Gardasil's five-year effectiveness span, yet infectious disease specialists and cancer pathologists say the incubation period for HPV becoming cancer is ten to fifteen years.

Most women are in their 40s and 50s when they are diagnosed, so the vaccine would offer no protection in the overwhelming majority of cervical cancer cases in the United States.

While every death is tragic, cervical cancer is fairly rare in the United States (each year causing an average of 3,700 deaths), only some portion of which are caused by HPV (and by HPV strains included in the Gardasil vaccine). As it is one of the easiest cancers to detect, chances are good of preventing death or other serious consequences. In developed countries such as the United States, where early changes on the cervix that could lead to cancer are nearly always discovered on Pap tests, the HPV vaccine will do little to decrease the already very small cancer rate. Women who do not receive the vaccine can still protect themselves equally well by undergoing regular Pap tests. In fact, if women who are vaccinated stop going for Pap smears, the incidence rate for cervical cancer will increase.

In the United States, the death rate from cervical cancer (3/100,000 women) is almost the same as the rate of reported serious adverse events from Gardasil (3.4/100,000 doses distributed).[5]

The vaccine is given as three injections over a six-month period at a total cost of $360 per child vaccinated, adding up to a $5 billion a year market for Merck Pharmaceuticals.

Do Vaccines Cause Autism?

Nobody knows what causes autism. Autism is a complex neurological disorder characterized by a range of learning and social impairments:

- abnormalities in social skills
- abnormalities in communication skills
- repetitive or obsessive traits.

Most researchers in the field believe the prevalence of autism has increased over the past two decades, but a minority says the apparent increase could result primarily from an expanded definition of the disorder and more of an effort to identify cases.

We know that genetics plays a role in autism, based on studies of twins and other family patterns: if one identical twin develops the disorder, the other has a 90 percent chance of having some aspects of it. And the sibling of a child with autism has at least five times the average risk of acquiring the disorder.

Many autism researchers believe that the disorder is triggered by a combination of an environmental factor and a genetic predisposition. Pregnant women, babies, and young children are exposed to an array of unnatural substances that may cause autism among genetically vulnerable individuals. There has been little progress in identifying what environmental factors—either before or after a child is born—might trigger the severe impacts to brain development seen in autism.

There are certainly many environmental contaminants that could be factors, such as air pollutants from power plants and auto exhaust, pesticides, heavy metals, and food additives. Other environmental theories include infectious agents, medications, vitamin and mineral deficiencies, and medical interventions such as radiation. Vitamin D deficiency caused by reduced exposure to sunshine or chemicals associated with indoor activities, such as household cleaning agents, was discussed in Chapter 10.

Mercury

Because childhood vaccine use and autism increased in the same era, thimerosal—which at one time was a basic vaccine ingredient—was often blamed for the condition. Thimerosal contains a form of mercury, which is a neurotoxin, and many vaccines contained levels that may have exceeded threshold levels established by the Environmental Protection Agency (EPA) when several vaccines were given. Vaccine manufacturers have reduced or eliminated thimerosal in childhood vaccines, which has reduced the infant thimerosal exposure by 98 percent, yet autism rates continue to climb. Also, while mercury is a well-known toxin that is highly dangerous to the nervous system, the symptoms of a person with mercury poisoning are *utterly different* from those of an autistic person.

MAD AS A HATTER

Mercury poisoning, once known as "Mad Hatter's Disease," relates to a disease peculiar to the hat-making industry in the 1800s. A solution of the metal mercury was commonly used during the process of turning fur into felt, which caused the hatters to breathe in the fumes of this highly toxic metal, particularly because the workshops were so poorly ventilated. This led in turn to an accumulation of mercury in the workers' bodies, resulting in symptoms such as trembling, loss of coordination, slurred speech, memory loss, irritability, and anxiety. The condition is most familiar in the literary character of the Mad Hatter, the madcap milliner in Lewis Carroll's classic children's book, *Alice in Wonderland*.

MMR

Thimerosal has not been the only area of concern in the vaccine-autism controversy. Based on a 1998 study, many people had come to believe that a correlation existed between the triple vaccine MMR (mumps, measles, and rubella) and autism. However, the gastroenterologist whose research had triggered the autism-MMR vaccine scare with this so-called study, which examined twelve such cases, has faced charges of gross misconduct before Great Britain's medical licensing board, the General Medical Council.

A Coincidence of Timing?

Many children begin showing signs of autism—around 15 months to 2 years—soon after many of them receive a series of vaccines, and that apparent link may just be a coincidence of timing, meaning that the two situations are related in time, but not in causation. For instance, symptoms involving delays in the development of many basic skills—the ability to socialize or form relationships with others and the ability to communicate and use imagination, especially in fantasy play—are often not apparent until after the age of 15 months, the age that the MMR vaccine is usually administered.

Too High a Vaccine Burden?

The FDA claims that their exhaustive reviews found no evidence of harm in the use of thimerosal in childhood vaccines. However, vaccinations have more dangers and more potentially harmful effects on the body beyond the mercury they once carried. Parents are worried by the sheer assault of multiple vaccinations all given at the same time and there are many scientists who persist with opinions about possible links between vaccination and autism, supported by various studies. It's clear that vaccines are not responsible for all autism, and not even most autism; but there are a few cases where the link has been assumed in the court systems[7] and so it is possible that vaccination may be one environmental trigger that can set off a cascade of genetically predisposed events that lead to autism, but the numbers don't suggest that vaccination is a major environmental cause of autism.

Vaccine Nation

American children are now the most vaccinated on earth. There are so many vaccines—most unheard of not that many years ago—but do we really need to immunize children against every disease on the planet? Most childhood infectious diseases are benign and end up running their course. Getting the disease usually imparts lifelong immunity, whereas vaccine-induced immunity is only temporary. In fact, the temporary nature of vaccine immunity can create a more dangerous situation later in life. Whether or not you decide to have your child vaccinated against any or all of these diseases, it is important to educate yourself about these vaccines and what they do, while you do everything that you can to keep your child healthy,

ANDREW WAKEFIELD:
THE CASE OF FALSIFYING DATA

After a two-and-a-half-year hearing, Dr. Andrew Wakefield and two of his co-authors were charged in 2010 with falsifying data related to the 1998 study linking the vaccine MMR and autism that was published in the British medical journal *The Lancet*. It is alleged that the children's conditions were not accurately represented, either before or after receiving the vaccines, and that he lied about the timing of the onset of autism symptoms as related to the administration of the vaccine.

There are also allegations about ethical violations related to the recruitment of child subjects and the performing of tests without proper parental consent. He also allegedly took large amounts of money from anti-vaccine interests in order to fund the study. The entire "research" was based on only twelve children, a tiny amount of subjects to have led to the worldwide vaccine controversy that exploded after the publication of *The Lancet* article.

Dr. Wakefield has no training as a pediatrician and had never been involved in clinical research before the 1998 study. His theory about the relationship between the vaccine and autism is somewhat circular. He has maintained that there are certain children who either because of genetics or some other reason are susceptible to a particularly adverse reaction either to live measles or a measles-containing vaccine, and that such reaction could lead to damage or infection to the intestine, leading secondarily to injury to the brain.

Ten of *The Lancet* paper's thirteen authors signed a formal retraction in 2004 after it was revealed that Wakefield was being paid by the lawyers representing families who claimed that their children had been harmed by vaccines. Then in 2010 *The Lancet*, in an extremely rare move, formally retracted[6] the 1998 study that purported to find a link between the childhood MMR vaccine and autism The British journal's decision to retract the research came after the United Kingdom's General Medical Council ruled that the researchers acted dishonestly and un-ethically, including carrying out unnecessary invasive tests on children and the aforementioned payment by the parents' lawyers. Among its findings on the study's improper practices, the council's report stated that lead author Andrew Wakefield took blood samples for research from children at his son's birthday party, and paid them each about $8.

---

to promote the strength of your child's immune system and avoid things that can weaken it.

Our bodies have the power and competence to heal themselves. Here are some suggestions for strengthening your child's immune system naturally:

- A fetus receives antibodies acquired by its mother from infections she's previously had. After birth, the best "immunization" a child will ever get is through extended breast-feeding. Breast-feeding provides multiple immune factors and optimum nutrition to the baby's body and brain. Continue for at least twelve months (go longer, if possible). The longer you breast-feed, the more your child will benefit. Breast-feeding prevents infections and the complications of childhood illness. Breast-fed babies are protected in varying degrees from pneumonia, gastroenteritis, botulism, bronchitis, staphylococcal infections, influenza, ear infections, and meningitis. Furthermore, mothers produce antibodies to whatever disease is present in their environments, making their milk custom-designed to fight diseases their babies are exposed to as well. Breast-feeding decreases a mother's risk of getting breast and ovarian cancer[8] and decreases the risk of her child developing diabetes[9] and allergies[10] and of her baby girl getting breast cancer in later life.[11] **If the government were to endorse a campaign to increase Americans' breast-feeding rate, and if the campaign were successful, more widespread**

breast-feeding would be a more valuable and cost-effective public health measure than all of the current vaccination programs.

- A healthy lifestyle continues the immunity established by breast-feeding. Excellent nutrition, avoidance of toxins of all kinds, exposure to sunlight, sufficient rest, and being part of a peaceful family all contribute to freedom from disease.

- Avoid partially hydrogenated fats (contained in packaged snack foods and margarines) because they promote inflammation and prevent healthy fatty acids from being incorporated into cells. Read labels of prepared foods and you will find that these fats are everywhere: in crackers, chips, cookies, and desserts. Avoid French fries and other deep fried foods from fast food establishments. Provide your child's diet with omega-3 fats that prevent inflammation.

- Avoid foods with added sugar, i.e., sugared breakfast cereals, sodas, cookies, and ice cream. Corn syrup is especially difficult for the body to metabolize. Corn syrup is everywhere, so read the labels. Use fruit spreads instead of jam, and use fresh and dried fruits whenever possible. Use whole grains and whole wheat bread rather than products made with "wheat flour," which means white flour. Use organic foods whenever possible.

- Do not give antibiotics or over-the-counter medications to your child unless absolutely necessary. They go against the body's natural ability to fight disease.

Now you know...

Every vaccine carries risks of harm that might outweigh any benefit derived from that vaccine. Weigh the likelihood that your child will be exposed to and then contract a particular disease and likewise consider any of the potential consequences of that disease. What you find out may lead you to question the wisdom behind some or all of the recommendations your pediatrician and other medical professionals make about vaccinations.

FOOTNOTES

1. Department of Health and Human Services Office of Inspector General Report, CDC's Ethics Program for Special Government Employees on Federal Advisory Committees, December 2009 (http://oig.hhs.gov/oei/reports/oei-04-07-00260.pdf).

2. Diekema, Douglas S., M.D., M.PH. and the Committee on Bioethics, "Responding to Parental Refusals of Immunization of Children," *Pediatrics*, May 2005, Vol. 115, Issue 5 1428–1431(doi:10.1542/peds.2005-0316).

3. *The Vaccine Handbook: A Practical Guide for Clinicians*, Marshall, Lippincott Williams & Wilkins.

4. Centers for Disease Control and Prevention (CDC) Recommended Immunization Schedule for Persons Aged 0 Through 6 Years (www.cdc.gov/vaccines/recs/schedules/downloads/child/2010/10_0-6yrs-schedule-pr.pdf).

5. Chustecka, Zosia, NewsMedscape Medical News, "HPV Vaccine: Debate Over Benefits, Marketing, and New Adverse Event Data," August 18, 2009.

6. Editors of *The Lancet*, "Retraction—Ileal-lymphoid-nodular hyperplasia, non-specific colitis, and pervasive developmental disorder in children," *The Lancet*, Vol. 375, Issue 9713, February 6–12, 2010 445.

7. Offit, P.A., "Vaccines and autism revisited—the Hannah Poling case," *N Engl J Med.*, May 15, 2008, Vol. 358, Issue 20, 2089–2091. Offit PA.

8. Rosenblatt, K.A. and D.B. Thomas, "Lactation and the risk of Epithelial ovarian cancer," *Int J Epidemiol.*, 1993, Vol. 22, 192–197.

9. Young, T.K. et al., "Type 2 Diabetes Mellitus in children," *Arch Pediatr Adolesc Med*, 2002, Vol. 156, Issue 7, 651–655.

10. Saarinen, U.M. and M. Kajossari, "Breast-feeding as prophylaxis against atopic disease: prospective follow-up study until 17 years old," *The Lancet*, 1995, Vol. 346, 1065–1069.

11. Freudenheim, J. et al., "Exposure to breast milk in infancy and the risk of breast cancer," *Epidemiology*, 1994, Vol. 5, 324–331.

Epilogue:
Peace of Mind
in the Pursuit of Happiness

"If there is anything that we wish to change in the child, we should first examine it and see whether it is not something that could better be changed in ourselves."
—C.G. JUNG

"The secret of health for both mind and body is not to mourn for the past, nor to worry about the future, but to live the present moment wisely and earnestly."
—BUDDHA

"Be the change you wish to see in the world."
—MAHATMA GANDHI

THERE IS NOTHING MORE IMPORTANT in the world than your relationship with your child. There is nothing more natural than to love your child, to be kind, compassionate, helpful, and nurturing.

Yet doing what comes naturally is not always easy. There are so many challenges in raising loving, peaceful children.

In order to make informed decisions you sort through the daily bombardment of opinions and advice from family, friends, and the media. You may be confused by advice from so-called "experts" or feel that your instincts cannot measure up to scientific and techno-logical conclusions arrived at by extensive studies and research.

Yet technology cannot improve on nature, and no expert on child-rearing can know what is right for your child. Doctors are trained to answer questions about sick babies, not where your child should sleep or how long he should nurse. You are the ultimate expert as you look for realistic answers to the question, "How can I raise my children properly?"

Any time that you try to conform to someone else's standards, any time that you have an automatic thought about what you *should* or *shouldn't* do to be a good parent, you are assuming something that might or might not be relevant to your own particular goals. A doc-tor's advice, or the rules of society, might have no validity for your own family's situation. Is it your priority to do what other people are doing, to conform to one's social circle, to do what the "experts" are saying? As long as others are doing it, must it be right for you? After thoughtful examination you might consider other possibilities and arrive at your own conclusions.

Stress

"Stress" refers to events that upset the body's physiological responses, all of which are geared toward maintaining equilibrium—a state of balance or harmony. A certain amount of stress is necessary in order for you to maintain focus, but chronic high stress increases your risk for depression. The antidote to stress is generally considered to be a sense of well-being, satisfaction, or peace of mind, all of which can generally result in a feeling of "happiness." Research indicates that "happiness" prolongs life and improves health. Happiness, in this sense, can be thought of as a feeling that your life has purpose and meaning. This involves such things as:

- Being engaged in activities of your daily life that allow you to develop your strengths and potential.
- Enjoying supportive and intimate connections with other people.
- Accepting yourself—your vulnerabilities and mistakes as well as your strengths and successes.
- Having clear personal standards that guide your actions and protect you from the judgments and expectations of others.
- Living your life intentionally, so that you are conscious of the moments of your life and grateful for the small blessings one misses without such mindful awareness.

Is My Baby Normal?

That is the most common question that pediatricians are asked. Despite what your pediatrician says, the correct answer is usually, "It's normal for him (or her)." There is a range of behaviors, sizes, temperaments, and development. The "growth chart," for instance, is based on averages, yet it is the rare child who is 50th percentile for both height and weight—in other words, "everybody but nobody."

One child might be talking at 15 months and another child, even in the same family, "doesn't talk" at 2 years. Yet the 2-year-old might have been riding a tricycle at 18 months. One is "a scholar" and the other "an athlete."

Most of the "out of range" behavior or development is simply "a variant of normal." Of course that does not preclude further exploration if the child is so far out of the normal range as to be a true concern. Sometimes, the decision to delve deeper into what might be a problem is mostly for reassurance, both for the pediatrician and the parent. It is never a mistake to ask questions and have your concerns addressed.

Finally, sometimes mothers have a "hidden agenda," that is, an underlying fear that is not verbally expressed. If such is the case, the pediatrician should be saying, "I sense that there's something that is worrying you that you are not telling me." Parents are often relieved to be able to discuss those fears and to hear the reassurance that usually follows.

Taking Your Child's Temperament

Temperament refers to individual differences in behavioral style. Each child has his or her own temperament. Temperamental styles are often apparent soon after birth. Infant temperament involves such things as activity levels, how fearful, predictable, and fussy the babies are, and their general dispositions.

During a doctor's initial hospital visit, newborns often respond in a certain way to various stimuli (such as being undressed and examined) that are remarkably predictive of the child's behavioral type many years later.

Specific markers of temperament include such traits as persistence, sensitivity, timidity, low adaptability, high activity, irregularity, irritability, and low *soothability*. Each of these traits requires that the parents respond in a particular way.

When there is a "bad fit" between a child's temperament and the parent's expectations of what "normal" behavior should be, this can lead to conflict. The parent or child might become frustrated; there might be tantrums, power struggles, and problems at school.

Based on nine traits identified by researchers (Thomas and Chess) in the 1950s, there are considered to be three categories of temperament:

1. **Easy or flexible.** These children demonstrate a steady, optimistic view of the world and are not deeply bothered by meeting new people or changes in their daily routine. Their bodily rhythms are largely predictable and they tend not to "overreact" to negative events or disruptive stimuli.
2. **Active, difficult, or feisty.** Children in this category are often labeled "fussy" or "a handful." They tend to have irregular eating and sleeping patterns, are resistant to change, and are fearful of new people. They are quite sensitive to noise, light, and commotion and react intensely to things that disturb them.

3. **Slow to warm, or cautious.** These children tend to be initially fussy and fearful but gradually warm up and become more comfortable with changes in surroundings, people, or events.

While understanding temperament is helpful in knowing the best parenting style for individual children, equally important is the concept that temperament affects the parents' view of the child and of themselves as parents.

Thomas and Chess developed the idea of "goodness of fit" to conceptualize how temperament and parenting may interact to influence a child's adjustment within the family environment. A child might be exuberant and extroverted in a household where quiet, calm behavior is considered the norm. Likewise, a shy child might be expected to be as outgoing as the other family members who see social reticence as problematic.

When parents do not understand a child's temperament, they might unknowingly squash that child's joy and inadvertently project onto the child a malicious intent, such as "he's doing that to get me." Most likely, the child has not a clue as to why the parent is getting upset. When parents' expectations, demands, and reactions do not fit well with their child's temperament, there is a "poor fit." A poor fit leads to a negative cycle in the parent-child relationship. Parents feel less happy and less capable in their parenting. The child ends up feeling bad by observing the parent's tone of voice and facial expressions.

Approximately 10 percent of babies and children have a "difficult" temperament. They cry frequently, are slow to adapt to new situations, and tend to have a negative mood. Parents of difficult babies may question their own abilities and lose confidence as caregivers.

It is helpful for a pediatrician to take the time to explain to these parents that they have a "difficult" child. Although the term sounds negative, it helps to use that word because it is the established term in studies of temperament and because it allows the parents to see their child as a "variant of normal" (mentioned above) rather than in any way abnormal. The term "difficult" is not pejorative or judgmental; it is merely descriptive of a child who is intense. The label explains to the parents what they are experiencing. From there, they can learn to understand how to better anticipate and react to their child without feeling overwhelmed.

No matter what the individual child's temperament, peace of mind is likely to result when parents can formulate an approach that creates a "good fit" between that child's personal style and his or her environment.

Move On and Let Go

In tackling the infinite number of issues that you will face as a parent, you will make some decisions that you will come to regret. While negative emotions are a natural response to what you might perceive as failure, it is important not to become so distressed that events of the past continue to cloud your judgment.

One possibility is to simply accept unpleasant and painful feelings such as fear, sadness, anxiety, anger, and disappointment. Experience the emotions for a time and then move on. There are so many daily frustrations. Sadness is a just a part of life and does not have to be seen as a negative emotion to always be controlled or eliminated. There is no happiness without sadness, no gain without loss.

> *Experience the emotions for a time and then move on. There are so many daily frustrations. Sadness is a just a part of life and does not have to be seen as a negative emotion to always be controlled or eliminated. There is no happiness without sadness, no gain without loss.*

Some mothers realize that some of their parenting choices could have been different or better, but they accept this and move on. Other parents regret endlessly. They continue to feel frustrated by what they believe has been lost, and feel pained and sad about it. A person can spend a whole lifetime grieving. Differences in background experiences and inborn disposition apparently allow some people to

Charlotte Yonge

recover from setbacks and others to become defeated. People who are typically more resilient also tend to be more optimistic, more confident, and have more of a feeling of control over events in their lives.

Whichever type of person you are, it is better for children if their mothers do not dwell on the past. Negative energy, guilt, and regret can only draw from the limited time and resources that you have in your busy life.

If you have had a negative experience, some tactics can help. Create positive options going forward. Focus on the important goals. "Keep your eyes on the prize," which is, ultimately, peace of mind and loving relationships. Find support among friends or professional counselors. Recognize that you do have some control over your thoughts and that you can train yourself not to "think too much." Don't keep replaying negative scenarios. You might not be able to get over regrets completely, but once you begin to divert and engage yourself, things will get better over time.

Outside Influences

There is always the temptation to blame another person for causing you to feel pressured and upset, as if that person had the power to take away your peace of mind. You start looking outside of yourself for someone or something that is the "cause" of your distress and you may become convinced that your unhappiness is the "effect" of other people's deeds: "It is your fault that I am not happy."

Peace of mind has nothing to do with other people or past events. It has to do with your own thoughts and feelings. What happened to you in the past no longer exists. All that remains are the thoughts, attitudes, judgments, and perceptions that you have about those experiences. You will always be unhappy if you blame other people for your unhappiness. Holding on to negative thoughts does not help you in your life. Anger, even if justified, does not bring peace of mind.

Your Parents

If you did not have the greatest of childhood experiences with your parents, you are not alone—all the more important to break the intergenerational cycle of poor parenting. People tend to repeat with their own children the very things that they objected to when they were children.

Most parents have good intentions, and few intentionally harm their children. Yet many parents make children feel that no matter what they do, it is never enough. Children become frustrated and feel bad when parental approval seems to appear and disappear without any knowable cause and effect. Many parents in decades past were taught to withhold their affections and approvals for fear of spoiling their children. Even though they might well have been attempting to do what they thought was right, you may still be working through the ramifications of this experience. When children are constantly trying to figure out what to do in order to get a parent's love, the resulting low self-esteem creates life patterns of poor self-confidence and feelings of inadequacy.

If this sounds like your parents, you can try talking to them if they are available. See if they honor your right to be heard. However, people do not change unless they want to, and you cannot necessarily change your parents. If you find that a parent questions your love, your loyalty, or your sanity, while telling you that your perceptions are wrong, then you might have to accept that they are just not capable of taking responsibility for causing you pain, and give up on trying to work things out.

Your parents are what they are. You need not carry a mental script for them that portrays the way that they should think, how they should be in your life, or what would make them happy. You can learn from their mistakes and move on.

Material Possessions Do Not Bring Happiness

It seems that much of the world spends most of its energy most of the time producing and acquiring more and more things.

It's natural to want to live a comfortable life, without struggling financially. Everybody recognizes the need for basic requirements: decent shelter, transportation, food, and clothing. However, when having material possessions and spending money becomes a passionate endeavor in and of itself it does not necessarily improve the quality of life. One of the most surprising findings regarding human behavior is that beyond the basic needs, accumulation of money and material things do not appear to provide a corresponding increase in satisfaction and happiness.

In short, as societies become richer, they do not become happier. In fact, the opposite is true. People in the United States, Britain, continental Europe, and Japan have more things than they did fifty years ago, but surveys show that they are actually less happy. When the purpose of buying material goods is to create self worth and personal happiness, it simply does not work. That is the paradox of living in a consumer-driven society.

Granted, money has power. With it, you can surround yourself with newer, bigger, better, and finer furnishings, clothing, and playthings. Money may also buy the envy of your peers or even fleeting friendship. Yet research has shown time and time again that what people need most, money cannot buy—the peace of mind that comes with moral values and meaningful pursuits, that it is better to be kind than to be rich. Also important are human relationships and freedom from the conflicts that could prevent you from enjoying what you have.

When people believe that their value is extrinsic, this belief can actually cost them happiness overall. If more income and more spending do not increase overall satisfaction, then perhaps a thoughtful review of your family's situation can weigh whether or not the acquisition of a certain possession will be worth what is being given up in order to get it.

Also consider what materialism does to the environment. Although we don't think about it too often, creating a whole new generation of super-consumers threatens our planet. Americans consume more paper, energy, and aluminum per capita than any other group on earth, and children have grown accustomed to a throwaway culture.

Every family represents a powerful force for positive change in their own lives and in the world.

Make an effort to escape the excessive materialism of our times. You need not purchase the latest toy, item of clothing, electronic gadget, or junk food. Children do not have to spend money that they don't really have or buy things that they don't really need. Don't raise children who define their self-worth through possessions and have little or no ability to delay gratification.

Provide a little shelter from the "more is better" culture and reject the idea of creating stressed-out "super-kids" who are overscheduled with competitive activities and whose success is measured by achievement of goals that are not necessarily compatible with basic emotional enjoyment. Look for creative ways to expose children to music, literature, the arts, science, and nature without spending a lot of money.

If individuals can change, then the course of the world can change. Parents can help their children reconnect to slower rhythms, non-material simple pleasures, and the experience of creative, unstructured free play. When a nurturing and loving mother is interacting with her well-fed, safe, and healthy child, their mutual joy and satisfaction show that opportunities for happiness are all around us, and that the ultimate goal of peace of mind is not as elusive as it often seems.

Acknowledgments

I could never adequately thank those colleagues, friends, and family members who have always been available during the many years that I struggled to organize a comprehensive guide for parents who seek a more natural approach to caring for their children.

My indebtedness to Charlotte Yonge, a Parisienne extraordinaire, is gratefully acknowledged. From her, I have acquired not only knowledge and insight but also unwavering support and encouragement. Charlotte is an unrelenting advocate for women and children, particularly in her roles as baby-carrying coach and La Leche League leader. She not only contributed extensively to "Keeping Baby Close–Carrying" (Chapter 3) but also kindly agreed to share some of the many photographs that she has taken of her own and other babies and children. These are included throughout the book. Charlotte's friendship and professional collaboration have meant a great deal to me.

Thanks should also go to my own children, Josh and Melody, who so quickly found the flaws in my attempts at mothering and helped me to enable them to thrive and grow into compassionate and capable young adults who I admire and respect. Ultimately, our children teach us everything that we need to know about being parents.

The book could not have come to fruition without the competence and cooperation of the entire staff at BenBella Books, all of whom have been patient and professional throughout.

Finally, my appreciation extends to all of you—interested readers who are patient enough to explore my alternative view, which is simply that the well-being of children often requires nothing more complicated than loving kindness, a peaceful home, and an acceptance of nature's remarkable ability to keep their bodies and spirits whole.

Index

About the Author

DR. SUSAN MARKEL is a board-certified pediatrician who has a private consultative practice specializing in attachment parenting and child health. A graduate of Tufts University School of Medicine in Boston, Dr. Markel became a fellow of the American Academy of Pediatrics in 1981, and an International Board Certified Lactation Consultant (IBCLC) in 1997.

For many years, Dr. Markel served as a medical liaison for the breastfeeding support organization La Leche League International. She is also a medical associate at Attachment Parenting International, a nonprofit parenting organization promoting "peaceful parenting for a peaceful world."

Dr. Markel has appeared on several live television broadcasts, discussing topics related to lifestyle issues, nutrition, divorce, stress, fever, and disciplining with love. She has been a regular contributor to BabyCenter.com and is a spokesperson for ERGObaby carriers, which features her on its Web site.

Dr. Markel divides her time between homes in Connecticut and Aix en Provence, France. She can be reached via her Web site, www.AttachmentParentingDoctor.com.

LINDA FOLDEN PALMER is a doctor of chiropractic, a consultant and speaker on pediatric nutrition and natural parenting challenges, a science writer, and a mother. She's the author of *Baby Matters*, and the updated and embellished version, *The Baby Bond, The New Science Behind What's Really Important When Caring for Your Baby*. She left her chiropractic practice shortly after the birth of her son, when she was confronted with his serious health complications and astounded by the lack of accurate or helpful information from doctors or books. For her son's sake, she delved deeply into the scientific and medical literature to find answers which led to further questions and some astonishing realizations.